HELPING
YOUNG CHILDREN
FLOURISH

Aletha J. Solter, Ph.D.

Shining Star Press

The sections on television in Chapter 3 are excerpted and adapted with permission from an article by Aletha Solter called "Television and Children" printed in *Mothering* Magazine, Volume #41, 1986. (Subscriptions: $15/yr. for 4 issues from Mothering, P.O. Box 1690, Santa Fe, NM 87504. Back issues: $3. All rights reserved.)

Shining Star Press
P.O. Box 206
Goleta, CA 93116
U.S.A.

Library of Congress Cataloging in Publication Data

Solter, Aletha Jauch, 1945-
   Helping young children flourish / Aletha J. Solter.
      p. cm.
   Continues: The aware baby.
   Bibliography: p.
   Includes index.
   ISBN 0-9613073-1-5 : $11.95
   1. Child psychology.   2. Child rearing.   3. Parenting.   4. Parent and child.   I. Title.
HQ772.S59   1989
649'.1--dc19   89-4229
                                                                CIP

ISBN 0-9613073-1-5
Printed in the United States of America

Acknowledgments

I would like to express my sincere gratitude to the many people who helped with this book. First of all, I am indebted to the friends and acquaintances, too numerous to list, who suggested that I write the book and who continued to encourage me once I had begun. Several people edited the manuscript and gave constructive feedback, including Gloria Berman, Pam Bury, Pamela Clark, Kathi Evans, Tonia Jauch, Pat Johnson, Hagar Kadima, Betty Pazich, Ken Solter and Rebecca Wave. I would also like to thank all the parents who let me interview them. (Their real names and the names of their children have not been used.) The excerpts written about my own children, Nicky and Sarah, are printed with their permission, and I would like to thank them for allowing this. I am also grateful to Phil Pazich who let me use his dot matrix printer to print out the first draft of the manuscript. Sam Solter and Nancy Solter Amodeo helped with the cover design and are gratefully acknowledged. Finally, this book could never have been written without financial and emotional support from both my husband and my mother.

"If we are to attain real peace in this world, we will have to begin with the children."

Gandhi

TABLE OF CONTENTS

INTRODUCTION

Since *The Aware Baby* was published in 1984, I have received many requests for a sequel. *Helping Young Children Flourish* is a continuation of the same approach to parenting described in *The Aware Baby,* and it covers the period between two and eight years, normally referred to as "early childhood."

You do not need to have read *The Aware Baby* in order to understand the present book, which is self-explanatory and complete in itself. If, however, you wish to gain a deeper understanding of babies' emotional needs, *The Aware Baby* may provide you with some insights and new information.

We need a new approach for raising children if we are to face the challenges of our complex and changing world. With so many problems such as hunger, pollution, oppression, and the threat of nuclear disaster, nobody can honestly admit that all is as it should be. Our challenge as parents is not to bring up children who will accept the status quo and continue the same mistakes of previous generations, but to produce a new generation of caring, confident, and smart people who will have the motivation, determination, courage, and skills to make this world a better place. It is time to question many of the currently accepted standards for treating children and do something different.

This book represents a new approach to parenting based on recent research and new insights into child development. It is quite different from most other books written for parents, yet it is the logical extension of current trends that focus on inner reality and feelings rather than external behavior and events. The approach can be started at any point in your child's development, and your child will benefit from it.

All parents want to have deep, meaningful relationships with their children and give them the very best upbringing possible, but this is often difficult to achieve because our society fails to support the work that parents do. The job of parenting is simply not valued enough, in spite of the fact that the well-being of future generations depends on it. Parenting is an extremely demanding job, and many parents are struggling under conditions of economic hardship, isolation, and physical exhaustion. All parents strive to give their children the very best, but parents are not given adequate support, training, or recognition. Parents are usually the first to be blamed for their children's faults, but are not acknowledged or congratulated when their children turn into well-functioning adults.

One way to make the job of parenting easier is to find other people to help you. You do not need to do the job alone. If you cannot afford to pay someone, perhaps you can trade help with other parents. If you are tired or sick, ask a friend or neighbor to come over. Do not wait until you are totally exhausted. You owe it to yourself and your children to take good care of yourself.

To help relieve the emotional burden of parenting you can take time to express your feelings. As you travel through the early childhood years with your child, you will experience many feelings, some pleasant and some painful. You may find that some areas of difficulty with your child are related to a similar difficulty you yourself experienced when you were growing up. It is perfectly normal for you to feel irritated, angry, frightened, or totally baffled by your child's behavior. But these feelings will need an outlet so that they do not interfere with your clear thinking about your child's needs and cause you to act in ways that you may later regret. One of the most important things you can do for yourself (and your children) is to find someone you can talk to about the feelings and concerns of parenting. If you are lucky enough to have a listener who can accept your anger and tears as well, that is even better. Expressing your own feelings in this manner will help you feel more confident and relaxed, and it will free you to become the kind of parent you would like to be. Take time to talk about all the daily irritations of parenting: the mud on the rug, the night awakenings, and the crying in the supermarket. The accumulation of these incidents greatly contributes to making our job as parents more difficult.

There are also deeper, sometimes overwhelming, feelings that we parents must deal with and express: Am I doing a good job? Will my child do well in school? Will my son have to fight in a war when he grows up? How will I ever pay for my children's college education? How will the world treat my child who is black (or Jewish, or female)? How can I prevent sexual abuse or kidnapping? How can I possibly fill all my child's needs, earn enough money to pay the bills, keep the house clean, do the laundry, cook the meals, spend time with my spouse, and help prevent nuclear war? And what about my own needs?

Following each chapter, there are three kinds of exercises that you may find helpful. The first are aimed at exploring your own childhood in order to help you become aware of both the pleasant and the painful memories of your own past. The second are to help you express your current feelings about your children. These first two kinds of exercises are in the form of questions to be answered with an attentive listener. The third kind of exercises are suggestions for ways that you can nurture yourself.

Until our society is totally supportive of parents, both financially and emotionally, we will find it difficult to be the kind of parents we strive to be, but we need not dwell on our shortcomings. Take time to appreciate yourself for all the good things you do for your children, all the hours you spend with them, and all the excellent thinking you do about their needs in spite of the hardships you are facing. You are probably already doing much more than you give yourself credit for.

WARNING—DISCLAIMER

This book focuses on the emotional needs of young children, and is not intended to be a substitute for medical advice or treatment. Many of the behaviors and symptoms discussed can be an indication of mental or physical illness, including (but not limited to) crying, tantrums, fears, laughter, sleep disorders, aggression, inability to concentrate, learning difficulties, eating disorders, bedwetting, and hyperactivity. Parents are advised to consult with a competent physician whenever their children display behavioral or emotional problems of any kind, or when pain or illness are suspected. Furthermore, some of the suggested methods in this book may not be appropriate under all conditions or with children suffering from certain physical or emotional problems. The author and publisher shall have neither liability nor responsibility to any person or entity with respect to any damage caused or alleged to be caused directly or indirectly by the information contained in this book.

CHAPTER 1: TEARS AND TANTRUMS

This entire chapter is devoted to the topic of crying: why children cry, the meaning and purpose of crying, research that has been done on crying, and parents' role during crying episodes. Temper tantrums are also discussed. Most books consider crying and tantrums to be "misbehavior" and fail to recognize the positive force that crying can have in young children's lives. This chapter offers a new way of looking at crying, based on current research and insights.

Why Do Children Continue to Cry After They Have Learned How to Talk?

It is quite baffling to parents when their young child continues to have crying episodes after she is quite capable of making her wants and needs known by language. As a baby, her crying was accepted because she did not know how to talk, and parents know that crying is a baby's only way of communicating her needs.

Crying is indeed a baby's way of communicating, and that is *one* of the reasons babies cry. But there is a second reason for crying during infancy which is usually not recognized. This is the kind of crying that occurs after all the baby's needs have been filled. It is common towards late afternoon or evening and can continue for hours at a time. It is the kind of crying that often worries and baffles parents because nothing they do seems effective in stopping the crying. There appears to be no way to make the baby "happy."

Surprising as it may seem, these crying episodes are actually healthy and beneficial because the babies are healing themselves of the effects of past distressing experiences. Babies accumulate many painful feelings even with the best of parenting. These feelings can result from traumatic birth experiences, inevitable frustrations, or confusion caused by limited information and understanding. Much of the crying that babies do is a tension release mechanism that allows these painful feelings to dissipate. (See my book *The Aware Baby: A New Approach to Parenting* for a detailed description of this kind of crying during infancy.)

The kind of crying that is a baby's way of communicating present needs gradually becomes replaced by language. The toddler learns to ask for food instead of crying when hungry. She learns to say "too cold" when the bath water is too cold. The need for this kind of crying therefore disappears. However, the second kind of crying that is the healing of hurts cannot be replaced by talking. Children continue to need to cry in order to overcome daily upsets and frustrations. They may learn to verbalize their feelings and say, "I'm feeling disappointed because Daddy didn't come home for my birthday," but talking about their feelings will only partially help children work through them. Children need to express their painful feelings by crying and raging in order to overcome them fully and thereby heal themselves of the effects of distressing experiences.

The meaning and purpose of crying have been greatly misunderstood. There is a cultural notion that equates crying with hurting, and parents are led to believe that their child will feel better if she would only stop crying. In reality, the opposite is true: *crying is the process of becoming unhurt,* and children will not feel better until they have been allowed the freedom of tears.

Most books written for parents list crying and tantrums in the section on discipline, along with other "problems" such as hitting, biting, foul language, lying, and stealing. This is an unfortunate attitude towards crying and raging, which in reality are children's most effective ways of coping with stress and keeping sane and healthy. In fact, it is often the case that crying and tantrums will help prevent or cure the "misbehaviors" with which they are so often listed. (See Chapter 5 for more on this.)

What Evidence Is There That Crying Is Beneficial?

Dr. William Frey, a biochemist at the St. Paul-Ramsey Medical Center in Minnesota, has researched the chemical content of human tears, and has found that tears shed for emotional reasons are chemically different from tears shed because of an irritant, such as a cut onion. This means that something truly unique happens when we cry. He has suggested that the purpose of emotional crying is to remove waste products or toxic substances from the body through tears, just as we remove waste products by urinating and defecating. The substances that are eliminated in tears are those that accumulate in the body as a result of stress. Some of these have been identified in human tears, specifically the hormone ACTH and the catecholamines. Manganese has also been found in human tears, an element that can have toxic effects on the nervous system if there is too much of it in the body. Dr. Frey's conclusion is that "we may increase our susceptibility to a variety of physical and psychological problems when we suppress our tears." In his studies of adult crying behavior, he has found that, in most cases, adults reported feeling better after a good cry (Frey & Langseth, 1985).

Crying not only removes toxins from the body, it also reduces tension. Studies with adults in psychotherapy have found lower blood pressure, pulse rate, body temperature, and more synchronized brain-wave patterns in patients immediately following therapy sessions in which they cried and raged. These changes were not observed in a control group of people who merely exercised for an equivalent period of time (Karle et al., 1973; Woldenberg et al., 1976).

Other studies have shown that therapy involving high levels of crying leads to significant psychological improvement. Those patients who did not learn to express their feelings in this manner during therapy tended not to improve, while those who did frequently cry in therapy made improvements in their lives (Pierce et al., 1983).

If crying reduces tension and removes toxins from the body, one would expect it to be related to physical health. It has been found that healthy people cry more and have a more positive attitude about crying than those who suffer from ulcers or colitis (Crepeau, 1980). There are documented cases of a relief of asthmatic symptoms and also a disappearance of hives when the patient begins to cry (Doust & Leigh, 1953; Graham & Wolf, 1950).

Prolactin, a hormone that plays an important role in regulating pregnancy and lactation, has been found to act directly on the tear glands and to play a role in regulating crying (Frey & Langseth, 1985). The more prolactin there is in the body, the greater the tendency to shed tears. During pregnancy many women find that they are more prone to crying than usual. Perhaps this is nature's way of maintaining mothers' bodies free of tensions and toxins for the developing fetus. Likewise, the increased crying that is so common during the postpartum period may be nature's way of maintaining the breast milk free of toxins.

A very small number of children suffer from a hereditary disease called the Riley-Day Syndrome (also known as Familial Disautonomia) which makes them unable to shed tears when they cry. When these children are experiencing mild stress or anxiety, their blood pressure becomes very high. They sweat profusely and salivate to the point of drooling. They often develop skin blotches, and some are prone to vomiting (Riley et al., 1949). It is as if their body has to compensate for the lack of tears by excreting toxins in other ways.

Work with severely withdrawn (autistic) children provides additional evidence that crying is beneficial. Several therapists have noted profound and rapid improvements with autistic children after they were allowed and encouraged to cry and rage during therapy sessions (Zaslow & Breger, 1969 ; Waal, 1955; Allan, 1977). In Janov's book *Imprints* there is a lengthy example of an autistic eight-year-old boy whose symptoms rapidly decreased once his mother began encouraging him to cry. In fact, the boy's progress was so remarkable that many doctors called it "unbelievable" (Janov, 1983).

The results with autistic children have been so encouraging that some psychologists have developed a similar approach to treating children who are extremely violent. These children are encouraged to rage and cry. Remarkable improvements have been observed after this kind of therapy (Cline, 1979; Magid & McKelvey, 1987).

These different areas of research all support the conclusion that crying is a necessary and beneficial physiological process which allows people to cope with stress. Crying can be considered a natural repair kit we all are born with. People of all ages benefit from a good cry.

What Do Children Need to Cry About?

There are many sources of stress in young children's lives, all of which create need for crying. Most parents find it much easier to accept their child's crying if they can understand the reasons for it. Unfortunately, young children are not always able to verbalize the reasons for their crying, so parents have no recourse but to guess. It is not necessary to know why your child is crying. The important thing is to accept the crying. Crying is beneficial whether the specific reasons for it are verbalized or not.

Some stress is caused inadvertently by us parents and other adults. Nobody is a perfect parent, and we all have our moments of impatience and unawareness with our children. This is because we all carry with us the effects of our own childhoods, and none of us escaped at least some form of hurt and distress as children. All parents are struggling to treat their own children better than they themselves were treated.

As you read through the following sources of pain and stress in young children's lives, you may find yourself feeling guilty about ways you have treated your children. If this occurs, you can try to focus instead on your own childhood, and on how *you* got hurt. There is no need to blame yourself, because you would not cause your children any pain unless you yourself had been hurt in some way. Furthermore, many of the sources of stress in young children's lives are not caused directly by anybody, but are the result of inevitable frustrations and growing in an imperfect world. Remember, too, that children can heal themselves of past hurts, and that you can help them overcome the effects of painful experiences, even those that you yourself may have inadvertently caused.

Many of these sources of stress in young children's lives have been studied by psychologists. If you are interested in learning about the research that has been done, a good review can be found in the article "Stress and Coping in Children" by Alice Honig (1987).

Hurts by commission. These are the hurtful things that are done to children by adults (or older children) who are acting out of their own pain, anger, insecurity, or anxiety. The major ones are being physically or sexually abused. Living with an alcoholic parent is stressful for children. Forms of verbal assault that are painful to children include being yelled at, teased, belittled, shamed, judged, labeled, criticized, humiliated, and blamed. Many children are exposed to racial slurs and stereotypes.

Painful feelings will occur every time children are forced to do something against their will or when their lives are overscheduled or overdirected. Misinformation is confusing to children. Punishment can make children feel anxious and unloved and can lower their self-esteem.

Young children are often messy, active, impatient, curious, fearful, and loud. These most natural behaviors are often difficult for parents to tolerate. Every time these impulses are reacted to with shock, disgust, embarrassment, impatience, fear, or anger (instead of with love and understanding) the child will feel humiliated and hurt, because a part of his real self has not been accepted. Many children are forced to repress these natural impulses, and therefore to deny their own inner natures in order to be acceptable to their parents. But they can never feel truly loved if they are treated well only when they are clean, tidy, quiet, passive, and patient.

Added to these hurts is the fact that children are not allowed to express the harm done to them, because it is so often done with good intentions and justified by being called "discipline" or "child-rearing" (Miller, 1984).

Hurts by omission. These are the hurts that result from a lack of appropriate behavior from caretaking adults, resulting in unfilled needs. Young children's needs are sometimes difficult to recognize and to fill. When needs are experienced but not filled, emotional pain and tension result. Just as with the hurts by commission, children can heal themselves of these hurts by crying and raging.

The major needs during early childhood are the need for adequate food, love, and plenty of physical closeness in the form of holding and cuddling. Children also need a great deal of individual attention from adults who are sincerely interested in their inner world and feelings, who can listen to them, believe them, trust them, and answer their questions honestly. Each child needs time every day with someone who thinks the child is important and special.

Children need a stimulating environment, a chance to be autonomous and participate in decisions affecting themselves, as well as a certain amount of access to the adult world. Additional needs are for freedom and space to play, and interaction with other children and caring adults. Children who must care for themselves after school for several hours a day may be under stress, even though they seem to be coping well. Young children need an older person available at all times who assumes caretaking responsibilities and provides companionship and emotional support.

Situational hurts. These are the hurts that are not caused directly by anybody, but by life circumstances. This category includes hurts such as physical pain or discomfort caused by illnesses and injuries. The death or prolonged absence of a parent is one of the greatest sources of pain for young children. The quarreling, separation, or divorce of a child's parents can also be a confusing and terrifying experience. Children's growing awareness of mortality, as well as observing violence or hearing about war, can be sources of fear and confusion. Children develop all sorts of fears, such as of abandonment, personal injury, or death.

In war-torn countries an obvious source of stress for children is the imminent possibility of being bombed or losing a family member. Other potentially frightening events for young children are natural disasters such as fires, floods, and earthquakes. Because of economic oppression, the living environments of many children are sources of stress. Overcrowded apartments and dirty streets, as well as high neighborhood crime rates, all contribute to feelings of anxiety. Even harmless events such as thunder and dogs barking can frighten young children, and trips to the doctor, dentist, or hospital can be terrifying.

Children who are in foster care can experience confusion, anger, and grief when they are moved to another home with different foster parents, no matter how loving the new parents may be. Less drastic changes in living arrangements can also be a potential source of stress for young children, such as moving to a new home, going to a new school, or acquiring a new stepparent. A well-known cause of stress is the birth of a sibling.

Even in the absence of any observable traumatic events, daily life for young children brings many frustrations and pains, simply because children lack information and skills. Children yearn to do what they see older people doing, yet often lack the ability. They develop misconceptions because of their limited understanding of the world. When things do not happen according to their wishes and expectations, the inevitable result is frustration, disappointment, or confusion. Because of an incomplete understanding of cause and effect and the limits of their own power, young children can develop guilt feelings for events that are totally unrelated to their own actions, such as a mother's miscarriage or illness.

Hurts carried over from infancy. In addition to the new hurts that occur during early childhood, most children carry with them stored-up feelings and tensions resulting from hurtful experiences or unfilled needs during infancy. Babies can heal themselves from these early hurts soon after they occur. If a baby has had a frightening birth experience, he will normally attempt to heal himself by crying as a baby. However, if his parents do not understand his need to cry, they will try to stop the crying by distracting him with rocking, jiggling, or a pacifier. Sometimes, because of exasperation and other people's advice, parents will leave a baby alone in a crib to cry. This is not helpful and will only cause new distress and fears for the baby to cry about. Babies need loving attention and physical closeness during crying episodes. The major sources of hurts during infancy (besides birth trauma) are unfilled needs, frustrations, and overstimulation. It is not unusual for a baby to cry for an hour or more a day, especially during the early months.

There is no need to worry or feel guilty if you did not accept your baby's crying and listen to him in this manner, because he can always catch up on his crying by doing it later, as a child. It is always possible for a person of any age to begin the healing process by releasing past hurts through crying.

What Should I Do When My Child Cries?

Most of us were not allowed to cry enough when we were children. Our well-meaning but misinformed parents distracted, scolded, punished, or ignored us when we attempted to heal our own childhood hurts by crying. Some of us were stopped kindly: "There, there, don't cry," while others were stopped less kindly: "If you don't stop crying, I'll *give* you something to cry about." Some of us were offered toys or food as distracters: "Have a cookie. It will make you feel better." (Now, as adults, it is not surprising that, for many of us, our first impulse when we are upset is to eat!) Another common approach was to send us to our room when we cried, which made us feel as if we were acting naughty. Many of us were praised when we did not cry.

In our culture, crying is even less acceptable for boys than for girls. Boys are often teased for crying and labeled "sissies." They are expected to "act like a man" and stop expressing their feelings. The consequence of this is that some men have not shed a tear in years. Perhaps this is one reason why men are more prone than women to stress-related illnesses and die at an earlier age.

Most of us got the message that crying was unacceptable. This led us to believe that a part of ourselves was not good, and we began to cut off aspects of ourselves in order to please our parents. We learned to hold back our tears, to deny our feelings, to inhibit the very essence of our beings. Now, as adults, many of us still cannot fully accept our strong emotions. Because we are not fully in touch with our own need to cry, there is a strong pull for us to stop our children from crying, just as our parents did with us.

With awareness of the importance of crying, and with conscious effort, it is possible to give our children the right to express themselves, even though we ourselves were denied this. A helpful approach when your child is crying is to say: "Go ahead and cry," or to acknowledge the child's pain by saying: "You're really sad right now, aren't you?" If you prefer to say nothing that is fine, too. All that is needed is to pay attention to your child by listening and watching, and to communicate love by your facial expression. If you are not comfortable with that, then you can continue what you were doing and smile at your child from time to time while he is crying, to acknowledge him. This approach is much better for your child than trying to stop the crying by distractions or punishment.

It is important to hold babies when they need to release tensions by crying. As children become older, it is not always necessary to hold them when they cry. Sometimes they need the space for vigorous physical movements while they are crying, and holding would only interfere with the process. At other times, they do need to be held, and will hang on, get as close as possible, and sob. Some children seem to resist being held, but do benefit from firm holding so that they can have something to push and struggle against while crying. On the other hand, there are situations in which moving in too close to a child will cause him to repress his crying. There are many different kinds of crying, and many effective ways of interacting with children that create the safety needed for the crying to occur. The important thing to remember is that children need to know that they are loved and accepted when they are crying.

If the crying is caused by a frustration, disappointment, or other situational hurt, all you need to do is acknowledge the child's pain and accept the feelings. The following example of my daughter illustrates how I dealt with crying that was caused by a disappointment:

> When Sarah was three years old, I bought a bathing suit for her at a garage sale, and I told her we would go swimming when the weather got warmer, perhaps in a few months. Later on that day the sun came out from behind some clouds, and Sarah immediately started to talk about going swimming, assuming we would be going that very minute. She had logically assumed that, now that the weather was sunny, we would go swimming, just as I had promised, and she could wear her new bathing suit. I explained to her that we were not going swimming, because, even though it was sunny, it was still winter, and we would get too cold. She looked very disappointed, did not seem to understand, and must have thought that I had lied to her or broken my promise. She did not have sufficient concept of time to understand what "a few months" meant. She was ready to burst into tears, so I picked her up in my arms and said: "You really wanted to go swimming, didn't you?" She sobbed heavily for a few minutes, and I held her until the crying stopped. Then she was as cheerful as she had been before.

In this example, it was clear that the feelings of disappointment were inevitable because of my daughter's limited concept of time. There was nothing I could do to fix things for her to make her feel better. Once I realized this, there was no point in distracting her away from her feelings, because they needed to be expressed and released. A young child's life is full of little upsets like this, and each one needs to be cried about.

If your child's crying is caused by something hurtful that you yourself have done (hurt by commission), then it is important to acknowledge your mistake, and apologize to your child, in addition to accepting your child's anger and tears. This may be extremely difficult to do at times, but it is very important for children to be told that they have been hurt or wronged, and that their feelings are perfectly justified.

A father I interviewed described the following situation with his six-year-old son:

> Today a friend called up and I hadn't talked to him for a long time, and we got into a great discussion right away. But right before my friend called I had arranged for Kevin to go over to a friend's house, so he was waiting for me to get off the phone so I could bring him there. I kept telling him, "Okay, okay, just a minute." And I really meant just a minute, but it was so much fun talking to my friend that I kept going on and on. When I finally hung up the phone, I went outside and there was Kevin kicking the ground and crying and he said, "You lied." So I held him while he cried, and he said, "But you told me we were going right away, and we didn't, and I waited and waited, and you still didn't get off the phone." It was hard to admit that I had lied because I sincerely meant just a minute. But once I understood his point of view, I realized that I was in the wrong, and I said to him, "I'm sorry, Kevin. I shouldn't have talked so long." With this approach I find that I get a lot more cooperation and respect back if he does something that hurts my feelings. He's very sensitive about that and he doesn't like to think that he's hurting me either.

There will be times when you will not know why your child is crying, and these outbursts may be the most difficult ones to tolerate. However, children need all of their crying to be accepted because there is always a valid reason for their tears.

What About Temper Tantrums?

Temper tantrums are nothing but intense crying accompanied by a lot of anger. Some crying is calm: the child holds quite still while the big tears trickle down his cheeks. Some crying, on the other hand, is very loud and powerful and accompanied by active flailing of arms, stamping of feet, or writhing of the entire body. We call the latter kind of crying temper tantrums, but tantrums are not really a separate phenomenon. They simply represent one of many kinds of crying.

The word "tantrum" can mean different things. It is used here to mean a genuine release of anger and frustration, a child's righteous indignation at having been hurt or wronged. There is loud screaming, yelling and crying, active movements of arms and legs, and real tears flowing. There is no violence or destructiveness during this kind of raging: the child makes no attempt to hurt anybody or anything. There is another kind of behavior that is often confused with genuine tantrums, which I call "acting out behavior." When a child is feeling frightened or angry, but not safe enough to express his feelings harmlessly in a genuine tantrum, he will sometimes become loud, violent, or destructive. He is acting out his feelings, rather than releasing them. This kind of behavior is often accompanied by loud screaming or yelling, as well as active movements (just like a genuine temper tantrum), but there are no tears. See Table 1 for a clarification of the distinction between acting out behavior and genuine release of anger.

If a child is not shedding tears, but merely screaming or yelling and hitting or kicking, parents can be helpful by realizing that the child is feeling upset, and trying to find a way for the child to feel safe enough to release these feelings harmlessly. Any hurtful behavior needs to be stopped, because no child benefits by being allowed to hurt or destroy. Sometimes firm holding of the child's wrists, or loving but firm arms around a child's waist, will provide a means of stopping the violence, and also of allowing the tears to begin flowing, so that the acting out behavior turns into a genuine release of feelings. Although the child may resist being held, it is important to continue holding so that the destructiveness is stopped. (The distinction between genuine release of anger and acting out behavior is not always clear-cut, as it is possible for a child to hit or kick while shedding tears. In this case, the violence needs to be stopped but the crying accepted.)

Table 1

Characteristics of Distorted
Versus Genuine Release of Anger in Children

Acting Out Behavior	Genuine Release of Anger
Loud screaming or yelling.	Loud crying, angry words, or angry sounds.
Violent and destructive.	Active movements, but no attempt to hurt anybody or anything.
No tears.	Usually accompanied by tears (or soon gives way to tears).
Occurs when the child does not feel safe enough to express the underlying feelings.	Occurs when the child feels safe enough to express feelings.
Does not resolve painful feelings: the child still feels hurt and tense afterwards.	Resolves painful feelings: the child feels happy and relaxed afterwards.
Firm and loving interruption can lead to a genuine release of feelings.	Interruption can lead to a repression of feelings.

Just as with ordinary crying, tantrums do not go on forever. Children stop of their own accord when they are finished discharging their pent-up feelings of frustration and anger. Most parents find tantrums extremely difficult to tolerate, because of the strong cultural taboo against such an intense display of emotions.

Some parents feel that their child is falling apart, going crazy, or out of control. Or they might believe the books that claim their child is spoiled because they have given in to too many demands. Parents are led to believe that temper tantrums are nothing but a manipulative device by a willful child engaged in a power struggle. Some parents are even convinced that temper tantrums are an indication of the evil nature of children, and should be immediately curbed before they get out of hand.

These attitudes towards tantrums are unfortunate, because they often cause parents to act punitively towards their child, who is only trying to discharge stored up feelings in order to keep himself sane and healthy. When tantrums and crying are not allowed, children can become depressed, aggressive, or prone to illness:

> The noted anthropologist Ruth Benedict had frequent temper tantrums as a child. Her father had died before she was two, and babyhood measles had left her partially deaf. Obviously, she had quite a bit to cry about, but her mother, not understanding her outbursts of rage, came to her one night with a Bible and a candle, invoked the aid of Jehovah, and made her promise never to have another uncontrollable episode of temper. Ruth's temper tantrums disappeared only to be succeeded by depressions. (Summarized from Moffat & Painter, 1974.)

This shows what can happen when a child's need to release anger is repressed.

Most books for parents suggest ways of stopping temper tantrums. This advice ranges from ignoring the tantrum to throwing cold water on the child's face. It is unfortunate that few, if any, books recognize the positive, healing nature of genuine tantrums, which are vital in helping children deal with stress.

Why Do Children Cry and Rage About Insignificant Things?

The length and intensity of crying spells and temper tantrums often seem to be unjustified by the situation that triggers them. A little girl screams for a half hour because she cannot find a picture she drew, or because you have served the "wrong kind of cereal" for breakfast. These examples do not seem to involve any extreme form of hurtful behavior from adults, and yet the children carry on as if their right to live has been threatened.

The reason this type of situation occurs is that children use minor pretexts in order to release feelings that have been building up. The "wrong kind of cereal" could be the pretext that triggers crying and raging about all the times that the child's real needs were not taken into account and she was not given what she wanted. Crying about a lost picture may in reality be crying about all the other losses that have occurred in a child's life.

Sometimes a child will cry for a long time when faced with a seemingly easy task (such as taking off a shoe), and say over and over again, "I can't do it." This is often baffling to parents, who know very well that their child is able to do the task. Perhaps this provides a pretext for the child to release frustrations resulting from not being able to do other things, which really were too difficult. This kind of situation is especially likely to occur if the child takes classes or lessons which demand a high level of performance, or if someone is frequently pointing out her mistakes.

The following example shows how children's expression of distress can be triggered by small events:

> A little boy screamed and cried when his grandmother came to visit and tried to hang her coat up in the closet. He screamed over and over again, "I don't want grandma to hang her coat in the closet." After crying about that, he finally said, "I want my Daddy" (who had been gone a long time). He didn't want his grandmother to hang her coat where his Daddy used to hang

his coat because he didn't want her to take his place (summarized from Janov, 1973).

The following example from my own daughter is an excellent illustration of a child taking advantage of a situation that allowed her to cry about a past hurtful experience:

> At four-and-a-half years of age, one day, Sarah had two bad falls: she fell from a ledge and also from a trapeze. Although I was with her when this occurred, I did not have attention for prolonged crying on her part, because I was dealing with other children at the time. That evening, when she was getting ready for bed, she was sitting on the bathroom counter next to the sink, after having had her feet washed. It was time for her to get down and brush her teeth. Instead, she began to cry, saying, "I can't get down. I might fall." There was a chair next to the sink, and she reached out one foot, easily touched the chair with her foot, but quickly withdrew her foot, claiming again that she could not get down, and crying about how scared she was of falling. I did not lift her down, because I knew she could easily get down by herself. She screamed and cried for about five minutes. Then she stopped crying, smiled at me, stepped down from the counter, and calmly began to brush her teeth.

This example shows how she was reminded of her falls that day by sitting on the counter and how she used the situation in order to cry about having fallen earlier in the day.

When children are feeling upset and needing to cry and rage because of accumulated painful feelings and frustrations, they will make use of any little pretext to cry. A mother I interviewed described this phenomenon with her six-year-old daughter:

> It'll be something that sets her off, like when I say, "No, you can't have this candy bar. It's bad for your teeth." She'll just cry and keep saying, "I want it." I can't reason with her. We get nowhere on the talking level, and she doesn't want me to hug her or anything. After she finally cries it all out, then I hug her and then it's okay. I usually realize by then that it's probably just pent-up tension. It isn't the candy bar or anything like that. It's just a whole bunch of stuff that she needs to get out. I try to be aware of that.

Some parents may feel that such a scene indicates that their child is spoiled or stubborn, or is purposely trying to aggravate her mother. Children cry like this because they are in desperate need of releasing painful, pent-up feelings. They are like a pressure cooker that needs an escape valve for the steam. You will not always know the underlying cause of your child's crying, but you can go along with whatever pretext she has chosen, and try to be accepting of the crying.

Will An Accepting Attitude Towards Tantrums Cause Them to Occur More Frequently?

(Reminder: The word "tantrum" is used in this book to mean a spontaneous rage reaction often accompanied by real tears, but without any destructiveness. Hurtful behavior towards self or others is not a genuine tantrum and needs to be stopped. This is further discussed in Chapters 5 and 6.)

A tantrum is a physiological discharge process very similar to defecating. When an accumulation of emotional tensions and stress is felt by the child, an urge to release by crying and raging is felt, just as an urge to defecate is felt when feces accumulate in the colon. To encourage this release and to pay attention to the crying cannot possibly cause crying to occur more frequently than normal, because, just as with defecating, when the child is done crying, there is no more. The release has occurred and he will not need to have another tantrum until his frustrations and tensions have again accumulated. To discourage a temper tantrum will lead to emotional constipation: a bottling up of feelings.

Some children become constipated and have a bowel movement only every three or four days because of a fear of using the toilet. Once this fear is gone, the child's bowel movements will return to a more normal pattern and will begin to occur more frequently. Likewise, children who have been made afraid to cry may begin to cry more frequently once parents make it safer for them to cry. It may look as if the parents are reinforcing the crying and causing it to occur more often, but in reality the child is simply displaying a more normal crying pattern because the crying is no longer being repressed. *Children do not cry any more than they need to.*

If you are still concerned about reinforcing tantrums by paying attention to them, all you need to do is make sure you pay attention to your child at other times as well, when no tantrum is occurring. This way, you will be reassured that your child is not faking a tantrum just to get your attention. It is impossible to fake real tears, however, and if real tears are occurring, then your child is definitely releasing tensions.

What If My Child Has a Tantrum in Public?

It is most embarrassing to parents when their child vents his anger in the supermarket, the park, or another public place. As children grow older, they do learn that certain times and places are inappropriate for loud behavior, such as tantrums, and they learn to control their outbursts. But every child needs to have at least one safe place in which crying and raging are totally acceptable and one safe person with whom tantrums can occur. During the early childhood years, children benefit by having contact with such a person on a daily basis. When this kind of acceptance and tolerance for tantrums occurs in the home, children will do most of their crying and raging in that safe environment, and will not feel the need to do so in public places.

You can learn to read your child's signals and predict a tantrum. When there are signs of imminent rage, you can avoid going out, if possible, until the tantrum has occurred. Just as you might see to it that your child goes to the toilet before leaving the home, you can also take steps to ensure that any needed crying has occurred. Some parents feel that allowing tantrums to occur in the home will communicate to their child that he now has permission to act that way everywhere. In actuality, acceptance of tantrums in the home will have the reverse effect, because the child will release his angry feelings in the home, and have no need to do so elsewhere.

If you wish to have quiet children in public, then you cannot expect them to be quiet in the home. The more a child can be himself at home and express all of his feelings openly, the more "well-behaved" he will appear to others when not at home. It is unrealistic to expect children to be quiet everywhere.

Even with a home environment that is accepting of tantrums, there may still be an occasional outburst in public. Most people are not shocked or bothered by such behavior as much as the parents fear. It is generally expected that young children will act that way at times (although the reason for crying is greatly misunderstood). There is really no need to try to stop a child's tantrum unless other people are clearly being disturbed. If you are not too embarrassed, a tantrum in public can serve as an excellent opportunity for you, as a parent, to model an accepting and relaxed attitude towards crying, showing other parents that it is not necessary to stop or scold a child at such times.

If your child picks a time or place for a tantrum that is definitely inappropriate, (such as in a restaurant, at a concert, or in a library or place of worship) you can take your child to the restroom, or outside to a place where other people will not be bothered by the noise. If it is impossible to remove the child, then you can do your best to hush him up by using distractions, if necessary. When a tantrum has been interrupted for any reason, it is important to remember that it has not been permanently stopped, but merely postponed. The child will need to complete the tantrum later. The sooner this is allowed to occur, the better off he will be, and the easier he will be to live with.

What If Children Have Learned to Suppress Their Crying?

Some children learn to suppress their crying at an early age because their parents do not understand their need to cry and attempt to stop them from doing so. With babies, many parents use pacifiers, jiggling, rocking, frequent nursing, and other distractions to get the crying to stop, thinking that the baby will feel better once she stops. The notion that crying must be stopped at all costs is so prevalent in our culture that some doctors even prescribe sedatives to reduce a baby's crying. The belief is that the baby would feel better if only she would stop crying. In reality, the reverse is the case: the baby will not feel better until she has had a chance to release her tensions through the discharge mechanism of crying.

With toddlers, crying episodes often continue to be misinterpreted, and parents are led to believe that their toddler is "spoiled" or "manipulative," when she is only trying to release tensions and frustrations. So parents feel it is their role to stop the crying, and are sometimes effective in doing so by ignoring it, or by using distractions. Many parents resort to bribes, threats, and punishments when other methods do not succeed in stopping their toddler from crying.

The result of this early conditioning to stop crying is that many children reach the age of two years with accumulated feelings and tensions, but with no acceptable outlet for them. Such children do not cry very easily or frequently because they have learned that it is not safe. They have often developed their own suppressing mechanisms to prevent themselves from crying in an environment that does not fully accept such behavior.

A common way that children stop themselves from releasing their feelings is by putting something in their mouth and resorting to prolonged sucking. This is typically seen in thumb sucking and pacifier sucking. Others appear to be addicted to nursing or bottles. Some resort to overeating, especially if feeding was a frequent response to their crying. Another common suppressing mechanism is to clutch or suck a favorite blanket or toy, typically known as "security objects." These favorite objects are held close by the children when they are feeling upset, but not safe enough to have a full cry.

Some children tense their facial, neck, and shoulder muscles in order to avoid crying, while others resort to self-stimulating activities such as head-banging, self-rocking, or masturbation to divert themselves from their need to cry. Those who are allowed to watch television sometimes come to depend on the TV as a distracter from their feelings.

These various suppressing mechanisms are called "control patterns," and there are many more kinds than I have mentioned here. Almost anything can become a control pattern if it is used as a means of holding feelings in instead of releasing them. Typical control patterns in adults include smoking, nail biting, drinking, eating, and muscle tensions.

In an extensive study of behavior problems of normal children it was found that thumb sucking gradually decreased between the ages of 21 months and 14 years of age. At 21 months of age, 21% of boys and 33% of girls sucked their thumbs, but none of the fourteen-year-old children sucked their thumbs. However, this same study found a parallel *increase* in the incidence of nail biting. At 21 months of age, only 5% of the boys and 3% of the girls bit their nails, whereas 33% of the fourteen-year-old boys and 22% of the fourteen-year-old girls bit their nails (Mac-Farlane, et al., 1954). It seems that, as children become older, they do not lose their control patterns, but simply modify them so they are more socially acceptable. Nail biting is certainly more acceptable for a fourteen-year-old than thumb sucking. Both behaviors serve the purpose of helping the child repress feelings in an environment that does not understand or accept crying.

Children who have learned to stop their crying in these ways sometimes display other symptoms that are the result of repressed feelings (Oaklander, 1978). Some children develop physical symptoms such as headaches, stomachaches, or rashes, while others become aggressive or destructive. Bedwetting can be caused by insufficient release of painful feelings. Some children become hyperactive when feelings are withheld, while others cut themselves off, losing the ability to concentrate or pay attention for very long. This is called "attention deficit disorder."

When parents become aware of the importance of crying, they naturally want their children to begin crying so they can catch up on the crying they needed to do as babies. The question many parents face is how to get the natural healing mechanism to function once again, and how to convince their child that she no longer needs to hold her feelings in. The task is not always easy, because it may take some time for the child to develop trust and feel safe enough with her parents to cry. The longer a child's crying has been repressed, the more difficult it will be to help her regain this natural healing process. However, it is never impossible to undo the conditioning, and the entire family will benefit when the child is encouraged and allowed to open up and begin releasing her stored-up pain and stress.

A first step to take in getting the process started is to begin paying attention to your child. You can set aside some time each day to spend with your child, being totally non-directive and doing whatever the child wants to do. Your child is not going to climb into your arms and begin crying. It doesn't work that way. She is probably going to want to play. If you are able to give good attention during these special times on a regular basis, your child will gradually begin to feel safe enough to bring up some of the things that are bothering her.

Children use their parents' attention in playful situations to help them work through painful feelings. The way they do this is often through laughter. Laughter is just as important as crying, and is a tension release mechanism that helps children overcome feelings of fear, anger, embarrassment, insecurity, and powerlessness. Since laughter is generally accepted in our culture and not usually suppressed, children usually feel safer to laugh than to cry. (See Chapter 2 for more about laughter.)

Your child may want to play doctor and re-enact with you a frightening visit to the doctor. If you go along with the game, you might pretend to be terrified of receiving a shot. Your child will probably begin to laugh, thereby releasing some of her fears. Or your child might want to play a board game and begin to cheat while peeking at you to see your reaction. If you understand this as your child's way of bringing up some feelings, you will not protest, but instead put on an exaggerated and humorous display of mock surprise at how quickly your child is winning. Your child will probably begin to laugh at this, thereby releasing feelings of inadequacy.

Puppets and dolls can be useful for children as a medium to express their feelings. Your child may ask you to take a role while she re-enacts a quarrel that frightened her. Talking and laughter can be encouraged in these situations.

This paying attention on a regular basis sets the groundwork for the next stage. If you have let your child take the lead, been accepting of her feelings, and encouraged laughter in these play-type situations, your child will gradually develop a sense of trust and feel safe enough to bring up deeper feelings with you.

The next stage is likely to be quite unexpected. Your child will begin to find little excuses for crying, and will test your reaction. This may or may not occur at times you have set aside for paying attention to her. A bruised leg during playful wrestling might cause a whimper. If you pay relaxed attention to your child at this time, she may feel safe enough to let the whimper develop into a full-blown cry. This is the beginning of the return to the natural healing mechanism, and your reaction is crucial when the process first begins to operate. Any negative comment or attempt to distract your child from her crying may cause her to close up again and continue repressing her feelings.

Unfortunately, your child will not always pick a convenient time, nor will her distress always look logical or justified. Your child may become upset at breakfast because you have served the "wrong kind of cereal." You will soon discover that nothing you do satisfies her, and your child will continue to complain. The most helpful approach, if this occurs, is to do nothing except pay attention to your child, because she is just looking for an excuse to do some crying. You can make it clear that there is nothing else for breakfast, and then welcome your child's angry crying. The breakfast cereal is probably not the real issue at all. You can go along with whatever pretext your child has chosen, and let the crying occur without trying to stop it. It may be difficult at these times to resist trying to "make things better" so that your child will be "happy." But you will probably find that nothing will make her happy for very long when she is needing to cry.

Once your child feels safe enough at home to release her feelings by crying and raging, things may become a little hectic for awhile, because she will make use of any excuse to cry. This is a good sign, although it may be a difficult stage to go through. Your child is not falling apart or becoming overly sensitive, nor is she becoming "spoiled" or manipulative. There is nothing to worry about because she is simply catching up on her crying that has been suppressed since infancy. Any crying that occurs is a tribute to you and to the good attention and safety you are providing for your child.

If your child still seems to be suppressing her crying after you have tried paying attention as described, then you can take a look at possible control patterns. Does she have a pacifier in her mouth much of the time? If so, then there is no harm in refusing to give her the pacifier, provided you explain what you are doing and why, and provided you are supportive and accepting of your child's crying. With thumb sucking, it is a little trickier, because a thumb is a part of the child's own body. The goal is to provide sufficient safety so that your child will no longer feel the need to put her thumb in her mouth. You can gently touch your child's hand when her thumb is in her mouth in order to draw her attention to it, while giving her your full attention. Children will spontaneously take their thumbs out of their mouths in order to cry if they are feeling safe enough. Do not give up if your child looks away or tries to push you away. It is normal for children to feel ill-at-ease and uncomfortable when receiving focused attention at times they are upset, if they are not used to this kind of attention. It is important to stay with them and keep paying attention.

If your child seems to have some embarrassment about crying because of other people's negative responses or teasing, you can suggest that the two of you practice crying together, and then create a playful atmosphere while you both pretend to cry. This is likely to make both of you laugh, and will help you and your child overcome some of the embarrassment about crying. It is important that your child understands she is not being teased.

If you yourself rarely cry, or if you feel uncomfortable around crying people, then your child is not likely to feel safe enough to cry in your presence, because she will sense your attitude. It will be helpful if you take steps to allow yourself to cry more, as described in a following section of this chapter.

Can Children Rid Themselves of Painful Feelings Through Artistic Expression?

It is a common belief that crying is an immature way to express one's feelings, and that more acceptable ways are through artistic expression. However, it seems that art work by itself, done in isolation, does not necessarily have any therapeutic value.

There is a documented case of a six-year-old girl who drew great quantities of somber pictures before she began therapy. Although she produced considerable art work expressing how she felt, this did not produce any improvement in her emotional well-being. In fact, her condition was worsening, which was the reason her parents brought her to a therapist. After a year of therapy, during which she had many long crying spells, her drawings spontaneously became more colorful and cheerful (Ude-Pestel, 1977).

It seems clear from this example that the drawings expressed how the girl was feeling, but were not, in themselves, therapeutic. After studying several famous writers who were severely neurotic, the psychoanalyst Alice Miller concluded that "the artistic expression of suffering does not do away with neurosis." Only the experiencing of anger and pain from one's childhood, and the freedom to express these feelings with an empathic listener, can bring about true healing (Miller, 1984). In a book that reviewed different forms of psychotherapy, the conclusion reached was that ventilation and catharsis (the full expression of bottled-up feelings) accounted for "a sizable portion of the total therapeutic impact of all psychotherapies" (Schofield, 1964).

Even though art work may not be therapeutic when done in isolation, drawing and painting can be a valuable part of therapy under certain conditions. Children's art work can be used as windows through which a therapist can gain access to the child's feelings. When the therapist accepts and reflects back the child's feelings, as expressed in the drawing, the child can then feel that her true self is validated and acknowledged (Oaklander, 1978). Once the child feels safe and accepted, deeper feelings can surface and tears can be shed. Drawings can also be useful in providing the therapist with a visual record of a child's progress.

I Find It Difficult to Accept My Child's Crying

Your child's crying may be very difficult for you to accept, at first. There are several reasons for this. In our culture, which has so greatly misunderstood the meaning and purpose of crying, we have all been conditioned, to some extent, to think of children's crying as "misbehavior." There are few, if any, people who reach parenthood having done all the crying they needed to do as babies and children. Instead, they were punished, distracted, fed, ignored, teased, or threatened when they cried. Although many people have been able to retain some ability to cry as adults, there are also many adults, especially men, who have not cried in years. The conditioning they received as children was so effective and so thorough that they have suppressed all crying. A consequence of this is a degree of denial and unawareness of their own feelings and a great difficulty to empathize with a child who is in touch with his feelings and actively expressing them.

Do not be surprised and do not blame yourself if you experience strong feelings when your child cries, such as anger, frustration, hatred, powerlessness, anxiety, or embarrassment. You may feel that your child is trying to manipulate you, anger you, or make life hard for you. If your own crying had always been lovingly accepted when you were a child, you would not be feeling this way. You would realize that you are not the target or the victim, and you would understand your child's crying for what it is: a necessary and healthy release. You would accept it as readily as you would accept your child's need to go to the toilet. A mother described her feelings when her children cry:

> If they are hurt or disappointed by someone else I can be patient, loving, and calm. If they are crying or raging at me in disagreement or to get their way, I get tense. These are the times I lash out in anger. I want things to go smoothly. When I get so involved and angry the kids aren't getting my focused attention, and then they often react strongly to that. It's hard for me to calm down once this has started, and things dissolve into mutual exchanges of anger and frustration. Eventually we calm down and talk it over and I apologize. I feel sad after these times. The kids don't always get their self images mended quickly, and the trust between us is strained.

In order to become more tolerant of your child's crying, you can take steps to retrieve your own ability to cry. You can begin by talking to your spouse or a friend about the ways you were stopped from crying when you were a child. If you feel a lump in your throat when you watch a sad movie, let your tears flow instead of holding them back. When you are frustrated or angry, hit a pillow and let yourself scream and rage. If you have had a hard day, ask your spouse or a friend to hold you and let you cry. If you are a single parent, call someone on the telephone and ask him or her to listen to you. Join a support group, or find a therapist that encourages crying. There are many therapies and growth movements that help adults regain the ability to cry. Anything you can do to increase your own crying will be very beneficial for your own health and well-being, and will also make it easier for you to create an atmosphere in your home that is accepting of your child's crying.

If your child's crying is really annoying you and you feel that you cannot tolerate any more, a temporary solution may be to distract your child away from her crying. You can suggest that you both take a walk, have something to eat, or play a game. When you use distraction in this manner, it is important to remember that the crying has not been stopped, only postponed. Your child will still need to finish her crying at another time when you or someone else has more patience and tolerance for it.

Changing generations of negative responses to crying can be an awesome and challenging task, but the results are well worth the effort and will be beneficial to both parents and children.

Is It Okay For Me to Cry In Front Of My Child?

Many parents wonder if it is all right for them to show their emotions to their children and cry or rage within earshot of the children. If you feel the need to cry when you are with your children, it is important to be aware of the manner in which you do this.

Children cannot be expected to play the role of counselor or therapist for their parents. It is unfair to ask this of them. If you need to cry, it may be best to do it alone or to wait until another adult is available to be with you, rather than expect your child to pay attention to you. If you do cry in front of your child, try to not put any pressure on her to listen to you or to sympathize with you.

Children may become frightened when their parents cry, especially if this does not occur frequently. They may need reassurance that you are not "falling apart," and will still be able to care for them. Guilt is another feeling that can occur. Your child may feel that she is the direct cause of your grief or anger. Even though something your child has done may have triggered your crying, she should not be made to feel responsible for your feelings.

Great care must be taken with expressions of anger. Yelling threats or obscenities and resorting to violence and destructiveness are not beneficial or therapeutic and are frightening to children. If you feel the need to yell or hit, this can be done into a pillow, as long as the children do not feel that they are the target. But be aware of the fact that a very young child or a child who has been hit by an angry adult in the past (or who has observed anger accompanied by violence towards others) may not be able to tolerate any expression of anger in adults, even harmless yelling into a pillow.

When done with awareness of these guidelines, crying in front of children can be a positive experience for parents and children, because the children will have a role model of an adult who can express feelings openly. They will realize that people of all ages cry, and that it is not a childish thing to do. They will see their parents open up and reveal their inner selves. This can help cement the bond between parent and child. Also, when parents have the freedom to cry or rage harmlessly, this will reduce the need to take their feelings out on their children. It is obviously much better for everyone when parents hit the couch rather than the child. The release of feelings through raging and tears will allow parents to become more loving and gentle and have better attention for their children.

Exercises

Explore your childhood.

1. What did your parents usually do when you cried as a child? (ignored, punished, distracted, comforted, etc.) What words did they use? What did they do when you had a temper tantrum?

2. Did you ever see your parents cry? What were the occasions? How did it make you feel?

3. Is there a traumatic event from your childhood that you still need to cry about?

Express your feelings about your child.

1. How do you feel when your child cries? What do you feel like doing? (This is not necessarily what you *should* do.)

2. How do you feel when your child has a temper tantrum?

3. Does your child have a control pattern? (blanket, thumb sucking, bottle addiction, etc.) How do you feel about this?

Nurture yourself.

1. Join a therapy or support group that encourages you to cry.

2. Every evening, with your spouse or a friend, take ten minutes each to talk, cry, and laugh about the upsets of your day.

3. Watch a sad movie and allow yourself the freedom of tears.

CHAPTER 2: FEARS AND FRIGHTS

Young children have many fears which are often baffling and worrisome to parents. The various possible causes of these fears are discussed in this chapter, as well as suggestions for helping children overcome them.

What Causes Children's Fears?

Fears are evident from birth on. Newborns are easily startled by loud noises and sudden movements. During the second half of the first year, many babies develop a fear of separation (separation anxiety) and a fear of strangers. These fears are normal and are considered an indication of a healthy attachment to a primary caretaker. Separation anxiety and fear of strangers normally diminish during the preschool years, but are often replaced by other fears. There are several possible reasons that can account for early childhood fears. I have grouped them into eight major categories.

Fears resulting from lack of information. Many childhood fears are simply the result of insufficient or inaccurate information. Much of the world must seem mysterious, confusing, and unpredictable to young children. Primitive people were once afraid of thunder, lightning, eclipses, and other natural events because they had no understanding of the physical laws governing these phenomena. Modern children are afraid of many things for the same reason. Anything that is not fully understood can be a source of fear, including toilets, vacuum cleaners, a wind-up toy, and natural phenomena such as thunder and lightning. Children continually form their own hunches or hypotheses about how the world works, but their ideas are sometimes incorrect because of insufficient information. A child might think, "If all of that bathtub water can disappear down that tiny drain, then I could too."

Fears resulting from distressing experiences during infancy. There is evidence that both prenatal and birth trauma can predispose children to certain fears and anxieties (Janov, 1983; Emerson, 1984). For example, claustrophobia (a fear of being in closed spaces) can have its origin in a long birth in which the infant was stuck in the birth canal. During infancy, babies can be easily hurt in various ways because of their extreme dependence, vulnerability, and lack of skills.

As mentioned in Chapter 1, babies have the ability to heal themselves of painful experiences through crying and raging. However, if a baby has not had opportunities to cry sufficiently with an adult's loving attention, the effects of these hurts will be carried over into childhood and manifest themselves in various ways, including anxiety and fear.

A fear of the dark may have its origin in the baby's cries having been ignored at night. A baby whose mother was hospitalized might, as a preschool child, have a fear of being abandoned. Insufficient touching and holding during infancy can also lead to nonspecific fears later on. Whatever the cause, any major hurt or unfilled need from infancy can play a role in producing fears in a young child, and these fears are often felt as life-threatening.

Specific fears resulting from current frightening experiences. A child who accidentally falls into a swimming pool is likely to avoid the water for many months, or even years. A boy who is pounced upon by a dog may become fearful of dogs. A nurse who gives a shot is likely to become a feared person. Although some feared events are dangerous, many of the things that children come to fear are not actually threatening to their survival.

Fears acquired by association (conditioned fears). Children can learn to be afraid of objects or events that have been associated in time with another frightening event. In a classical experiment done in 1920, an eleven-month-old boy called Albert was happily playing with a white rat. Suddenly, the experimenter struck a suspended steel bar with a hammer to produce a loud, startling noise. The bar was struck a total of seven times while Albert played with the rat. Following this, Albert was quite afraid of the rat, and shrunk away in fear when he saw it, even though the rat itself had not hurt him. The fear also spread to other, similar objects, such as a rabbit, dog, fur coat, and cotton wool. Albert expressed fear and avoidance when shown those objects, which had previously not frightened him in the least (Watson & Rayner, 1920).

These fears are called "conditioned fears," and the phenomenon of a conditioned fear spreading to other similar objects is called "generalization." Many of the fears of preschool aged children are the result of conditioning and generalization. The frightening event need not be a loud gong. Anything that frightens a child can cause a fear of objects or events occurring at the same time, by simple association: a dog barking, thunder, a toilet overflowing, a sudden stop in a car, or a siren from a fire-engine. If a girl is happily playing naked in a wading pool when a sudden clap of thunder occurs she may be afraid to play in the wading pool from then on. This fear can spread to all wading pools, to all water play, or to a fear of being nude.

Fears acquired from other people. Children can easily "catch" fears from their parents. If a father sees a spider in the house and makes a sudden movement with a startled exclamation, a child nearby may develop a fear of spiders from that incident. The child has not been initially frightened by the spider, but by her father's *reaction* to the spider. It is frightening and confusing to a young child when a trusted adult acts in an unexpected or unpredictable manner, especially if it involves a sudden withdrawal of attention from the child or an unusual sound. Seeing the spider at the same time as her father's reaction, the child may then come to fear spiders by simple association, just as little Albert came to fear rats. The fear may then spread to all small, bug-like creatures.

Parents can unknowingly pass on their own fears to their children in this manner, because the parents' fear itself is distressing to the child. Here is my own experience with this:

> At two years of age, Nicky developed a fear of things blowing away in the wind, because I once overreacted and suddenly became frantic when some important papers of mine started blowing away. My reaction must have startled him, because I had suddenly switched from a calm mother to a hysterical one. For several months afterwards, he panicked, screamed, and cried when the wind came up in our back yard and blew his things around.

The evolutionary advantage of such a mechanism of fear contagion is obvious. Children survived better if they could quickly and effectively acquire their parents' fears of dangerous animals, places, or events. It is quite likely that many of children's fears are of this nature, and that many of our adult fears had a similar origin in our own childhoods.

Fears and prejudices towards other people or races can have their origin through this same mechanism of conditioned fear caused by the parent's own reaction. If a white mother has a fear or distrust of black people, her child will sense this fear each time they see a black person. Perhaps the mother holds the child's hand more tightly, acquires a sudden, fearful look in her eyes, or shows a lapse of attention. These reactions, although subtle, can frighten and confuse a child, and the child can come to fear black people by associating them with her mother's tense or strange behavior. Even though no derogatory remarks are made about other races, and even though the parents may claim to be non-racist, children can readily acquire whatever unconscious prejudices their parents are harboring by assimilating these nonverbal cues.

If the parents are overly anxious about their child's health or safety, the child can readily acquire these same fears, which are transmitted partly through the process of conditioning, as described above, and partly through misinformation given to the child. For example, if a mother is overly concerned with cleanliness, she may become startled or angry when her child's hands are dirty, thereby frightening the child by her reaction. At the same time, she may give misinformation, such as, "Don't ever touch dirt. It can make you sick." The information can also be conveyed nonverbally. Perhaps she insists on washing the child's hands more than necessary.

Parents can unknowingly cause fears in their children in other ways. If the children are frequently punished or made to feel guilty for doing the things that children normally do (such as being loud, messy, or curious), then general fearfulness can develop. Also, when children's feelings are not fully accepted (as described in Chapter 1) children may come to feel that their whole selves have not been totally accepted. This can help contribute to fears of being abandoned because, in a sense, a part of their being has indeed been abandoned.

Children also acquire fears from sources other than their parents. Young children are very trusting, and tend to believe everything they hear. If someone tells a little boy that his penis will fall off if he touches it, he may believe this and develop a fear of losing his penis. Books, movies, and television programs can also be sources of new fears.

Fears resulting from a growing awareness of death. Babies live in a blissful state in which they have no awareness of their own mortality. Although they know very well what they need in order to survive, and although they experience distress when their well-being and existence are threatened, they do not have a conscious understanding of the concept of death.

Around the age of three children begin to develop a new awareness of death and of their own vulnerability and mortality. This is made evident by their questions such as, "Will I die?", "Will you die?", and "Why do people die?" This awareness of death can cause new fears to appear around this age. A boy who has had no hesitation about being in a dark room may suddenly refuse to stay in the dark. A little girl may begin to resist taking a bath for fear of going down the drain with the bath water. Another child may suddenly dislike a story about monsters that used to be a favorite. Fears of being kidnapped or abandoned can arise during the preschool years because of this new awareness of vulnerability.

Fears resulting from the child's growing imagination. In addition to a new knowledge of the possibility of death, children of this age have a vivid imagination. Their ability to use symbolic thought, such as mental imagery and language, increases rapidly during the preschool years (Piaget, 1962). This ability allows them to expand their thought processes to include events removed in time or space from the present moment, and even to visualize events entirely of their own creation. Until young children acquire more knowledge of the real world, the distinction between reality and their own fantasies is not always clear. Events quite insignificant to adults can be magnified out of proportion and become sources of considerable anxiety. I observed this with my daughter:

> When Sarah was little, I used to hold her in my arms in the evening until she fell asleep. One evening, just a few weeks before her third birthday, she suddenly said, "I don't like the curtains." It seems that she was afraid of the shadows thrown on the curtains from the bushes and the street light outside. The shadows looked like huge animals. She requested a light on in the room, something she had never wanted before, even though these curtains and shadows had always been there. About a week after this, she asked her first question about death: "What can dead people do?"

Symbolic fears. Symbolic fears are specific fears that can arise when there is a threatening event that a child is unable to verbalize. The birth of a younger sibling may cause a young child to develop a new fear of a monster hiding in her closet. The real fear is a deep-seated anxiety about losing her parents' love. The child's mind, unable to pinpoint or deal with this overwhelming anxiety, focuses the fear onto an imagined monster. She can verbalize this fear, thereby communicating to her parents that something is bothering her. The fear is symbolic, because it represents, or takes the place of, another, less well-definable fear.

Symbolic fears can also arise during an impending divorce by the parents, during a parent's illness, or following sexual abuse. Whenever it is too difficult or unsafe for a child to express the real fear, then symbolic fears are likely to develop.

Monsters can be a general symbol for any adult irrationality. When a parent suddenly becomes impatient and yells, or slaps a child, this can be terrifying and confusing. From the child's point of view, parents who act in these ways are indeed behaving like monsters. They are no longer the loving, predictable humans they were a minute ago. Since none of us parents are perfect, all children experience occasional hurts of these types. Perhaps the universal evil characters, such as trolls, monsters, and witches found in fairy tales throughout the world, are meaningful to children because they represent the irrational and hurtful side of the adults with whom the children live (Bettelheim, 1975).

What Fears Are the Most Common?

Whatever the cause, most children between the ages of two and eight years have some fears, and each child develops her own personal ones, based on her temperament, imagination, life circumstances, and experiences. In spite of individual differences, there seem to be certain fears that are more common than others. The most common fears of young children are of animals (especially dogs and snakes), doctors, storms, darkness, strangers, unfamiliar situations, and imaginary creatures (Miller et al., 1972).

Children who had strong separation anxiety as babies have been found to be more fearful as well during the preschool years (Newson & Newson, 1968). Some children have more vivid imaginations and dwell more on possibilities than others. In those children, fears are likely to be more intense than in others. Boys who are more aware of and sensitive to visual novelty as babies are more fearful later on, although this is not the case for girls (Bronson, 1970).

Fears are not logical and do not respond to logic or reason. It is not at all uncommon for a child to be terrified of quite innocuous things, such as the bathtub drain, while at the same time showing no fear whatsoever of real potential threats to her safety, such as traffic or germs (Maurer, 1965). This can be quite disconcerting for parents, as well as frustrating, because of the failure of adult logic to dispel children's fears.

In spite of their irrationality and intensity, early childhood fears are usually considered to be a normal part of development, and are not an indication of psychopathology (even though fears of a similar intensity in adults might be considered pathological). Early fears are not necessarily associated with other problems, and they are not predictive of emotional disorders in adulthood (Rutter, 1975). It is easy for parents to assume that their child is severely disturbed when this may not be the case at all. Your fearful child will not necessarily grow into a phobic adult.

How Should I React When My Child Expresses a Fear?

Before I discuss helpful ways to respond to children's fears, I would like to mention some ways that are not helpful. Sometimes an older child or even an adult will tease a younger child about his fears. All forms of teasing are cruel and damaging. Teasing is especially likely to occur if the older person has been teased himself, or feels the need to prove himself better than the younger one. Teasing will not make fears go away. On the contrary, it will only create more painful feelings for the child to deal with. Teasing also destroys trust and safety. A child who has been teased will be much less likely to admit fears in the future, but he will not *be* any less fearful. He will simply keep his fears to himself.

A common mistaken approach by well-intentioned parents is to protect a child from the objects or events he is afraid of. Parents may stop going to the beach if their child is afraid of the ocean, avoid going to the zoo if he has a fear of animals, or stay away from a friend's house that has a dog. They may even refrain from bathing a young child who is terrified of bathtubs. Although this appears to be a loving and humane way of treating a fearful child, such an approach will not help the child overcome his fears.

Children do need to be protected from real potential threats to their physical safety, but they do not need to be protected from imagined dangers. To do so will only confuse them and may even further contribute to their fears. A child may think that there must be real danger if his parents keep him away from certain places.

Some parents go to the other extreme and, in their eagerness for their children to have enjoyable experiences, force their children to confront fearful situations without any awareness of or attention to the children's feelings. I have seen many young children plunged into a swimming pool against their will or forced to sit on Santa Claus's lap for a photograph, in spite of loud protests. The child is expected to be tough or brave, and any display of fear is discouraged. These experiences can be overwhelming to children and can lead to feelings of anger and resentment.

Even when force is not used, parents are sometimes less helpful than they could be because of their failure to acknowledge and accept the child's feelings. Because of a desire to reassure a frightened child, it is very tempting to say, "There's nothing to be afraid of," or "Don't be scared." Such statements deny the reality of the child's experience and feelings. There obviously is something to be afraid of, or the child would not be afraid! When parents tell a child to be brave, the child may begin to feel that there is something wrong with him for having the fear. Not only that, his parents' denial and dismissal of his fear let him know that they are unable to help him overcome it. The child is left with the same fear still there, but, in addition, feelings of shame, loneliness, and hopelessness. A child who feels safe enough to express the fact that he is afraid is asking for help. He does not need someone telling him he should not be feeling that way.

A first step, even if you do not know how to help your child with a specific fear, is to *acknowledge* the fear, and to offer sympathy and hope. For example, "I can see that you are very scared of the ocean, and it's not fun being that scared, is it? Maybe together we will figure out a way to help you get over your fear, so that we can enjoy going to the beach again." By saying this, you are letting your child know you understand how he must be feeling, and that you are willing to help him overcome the fear.

You can do much more than acknowledge your children's fears. You can actively help your child overcome his fears by using certain therapeutic techniques in the home based on current research, as the following sections describe.

What Has Research Shown About Overcoming Fears?

In Chapter 1, the beneficial effects of crying and raging were described. These forms of release, often accompanied by trembling, can be helpful in overcoming heavy fears. However, there is another tension-release mechanism that plays a particularly important role in helping people of all ages overcome fears. This is laughter. People often laugh when they are feeling frightened, startled, or embarrassed. Jokes that make us laugh usually involve an element that is incongruous with our expectations, or they deal with embarrassing topics such as sex or nudity, or make reference to death. Comical films such as those by Charlie Chaplin involve embarrassing situations. Famous comedians and clowns are actually very astute therapists, since they are able to bring up people's fears and embarrassments in a way that is not threatening and that allows people to release tensions by means of laughter.

The ability of laughter to reduce tension has been demonstrated in a scientific study (Bushnell, 1979), and laughter is gradually being recognized as an important factor in maintaining physical health, especially since Norman Cousins cured himself from a serious disease using laughter and vitamin C (Cousins, 1979).

Throughout the ages, laughter has been used successfully by shamans (medicine men), clowns, and court jesters to cure people of fears as well as depressions (Moody, 1978). In modern times, laughter has been shown to be helpful in dealing with fears by a number of different therapists. In a therapeutic approach called "paradoxical intention" laughter is a major component of therapy, and has been found to be quite effective in curing phobias

(Frankl, 1967). Several other examples of the uses of laughter in psychotherapy are mentioned in a book called *Humor and Psychotherapy* (Kuhlman, 1984). Laughter therapy has been shown to be effective with children as well (Loewald, 1976).

A method of fear therapy called "systematic desensitization" does not claim to be a method using laughter, but it is likely that laughter occurring spontaneously accounts for at least a part of its effectiveness. The original idea of systematic desensitization was to have the patient gradually imagine a fear-producing stimulus, while maintaining a state of relaxation, until the stimulus no longer aroused a fear response. The theory claimed that the stimulus would become associated with relaxation instead of with physiological arousal (that is, fear) (Lazarus, 1960). Although systematic desensitization does work in many cases, it is interesting that relaxation is not a necessary factor for success. Some therapists have discovered that producing laughter with the use of humorous visual images is even more effective than trying to get the patient to relax (Ventis, 1973; Smith, 1973). When traditional desensitization therapy is used with young children, it has been found that relapses are fairly common (Gelfand, 1978). Perhaps with encouragement of laughter, the therapy would be more effective with young children.

As mentioned above, crying and shaking are also beneficial, especially for heavy fears. In the "Implosive Technique," the therapist typically describes scenes related to the patient's phobia. It has been observed that, during this kind of therapy, there is a good deal of emotional discharge. The patients shudder in fear, cry out in anger, or shed copious tears. It has even been suggested and shown experimentally that, far from being incidental, the violent emotional experience is a necessary and integral part of the therapy (Hodgson & Rachman, 1970).

A common element in many of these therapeutic techniques is to expose the patient to the feared object (in small doses, or symbolically), and to allow the patient to release feelings, either through laughter, crying, or trembling.

How Can I Help My Children Overcome Their Fears?

There are two important steps you can take as a parent when faced with the reality of a child's fears: 1) Give your child accurate information, and 2) Encourage your child to release her feelings by laughing. (For heavy fears, crying and shaking may be necessary as well, in order to fully release the feelings.)

Give your child accurate information. Many fears result from insufficient or inaccurate information, as described in a previous section. Much of the world must seem mysterious and confusing to young children. Once they have a better understanding of how and why things work, many of their fears will simply disappear:

> When Sarah developed a fear of the curtains at night, because of the large, strange-looking shadows on them, I showed her the street light (the source of light), and the bushes by the window that were casting the shadows. We looked at them and talked about them, both during the daytime and after dark. For several days, she kept pointing out the street light and commenting on it to anyone who was around. After that, she no longer seemed as afraid of the curtains at night, and even said, "I like the curtains now."

Children sometimes fear bodily harm because of an insufficient understanding of physiological processes. A little boy was terrified of bleeding to death from a scratch, but once he understood about the coagulation of blood and scab formation, his fears subsided. Another was afraid of urinating because he thought his insides would fall out if he "let the cork out." After some basic anatomy was explained to him, he was quite relieved (Joseph, 1974).

Children acquire or invent mistaken notions about all sorts of things. The importance of continually providing correct and accurate information cannot be overemphasized. Children need information about their own bodies and about household devices such as toilets and vacuum cleaners. They need to hear correct facts about animals: which ones sometimes attack humans and why, and which ones do not. They need to hear the truth about death, and the difference between sleep and death. They also need to have clear distinctions made between reality and fantasy, to know that witches, ghosts, and monsters do not exist, and that nobody has super powers, either good or evil. This information is especially important if the child watches television.

Children also benefit immensely from explanations about natural phenomena such as fire, thunder, lightning, tornados, tides, and earthquakes. Most importantly, children need correct information about human distress and the causes of violence. They need to be told that when people hurt each other it is not because they are "bad" or "evil" but only because they are feeling hurt and scared. All of this information can be supplied casually in the context of the child's own questions, without denying or dismissing any fears the child may already have.

Sometimes information does not help because the child is not ready to understand or to believe the explanations. Preschool children do not yet have the reasoning ability required to understand all of the cause-and-effect relationships and physical laws that adults take for granted (Piaget, 1950). A fear of going down the bathtub drain may persist until the child has a clear understanding of the difference between solid and liquid states. It is sometimes necessary to wait for the child's brain to mature and for specific learning experiences to occur before certain fears can be overcome. Many of children's fears simply disappear of their own accord, without any treatment at all (Miller et al., 1972). I observed this in my son:

> At two years of age, Nicky was afraid to put his beach ball in the neighborhood wading pool for fear it would disappear down the filter drain, an impossible event. No amount of explanations seemed to help this fear subside. When he was seven years of age, we returned to our old neighborhood and visited the wading pool, after not having been there for several years. He said, "Remember when I was afraid of my ball going down that drain?" He seemed very amused at the fact that he had once been afraid of such a ridiculous thing.

Giving children information that allows them to anticipate and predict what will happen in a frightening situation can also be helpful. This approach can be used when you will be doing something with your child that you suspect will frighten her, such as visiting a doctor. Children can also benefit from learning about and practicing specific coping strategies. If your child is afraid of dogs, you can help her feel more confident by rehearsing different things she can do if she sees a dog, such as hold somebody's hand, slowly back away, or call for help (Hyson, 1986).

Encourage a release of feelings. In the case of fears resulting from a traumatic experience, it is important to encourage a release of feelings as soon as possible after the frightening event has occurred. A distressing experience will result in a lasting fear only if the child is not able to release her feelings about the event at the time.

If a child falls into a swimming pool and is then allowed to cry, shake, laugh, and talk about the experience as long as needed, she will be no more afraid of swimming pools than she was before she fell in. She might become more *careful*, but she will not be *fearful*. She will take the necessary precautions to avoid falling in again, but she will not experience the physiological reactions associated with fear (such as increased heart rate and shortness of breath). Her body will not mobilize its defenses against danger because her mind will realize that there is no danger, as long as she does not go too near the edge.

If a child has not had sufficient opportunity to discharge the feelings immediately following a traumatic event, she can always do so later. A mother reported to me how her eight-year-old son was able to overcome a fear of deep water by crying about an event that had happened to him three years previously. Here is her story:

> When Tom was five years old, I let him take a swimming lesson from someone who was training to become a swim instructor. She was very eager to teach him how to do things in the water. Well, Tom was flabbergasted when he saw that Olympic-sized

pool, and when he realized that the water was too deep for him to stand in. The teacher put pressure on him to get in, and when he didn't do so, she just carried him into the water. When he said, "I'm ready to get out now," she said, "Oh, no, Tom. You're not ready to get out," and kept him in the water against his will. He didn't cry much at the time. It wasn't a safe situation. He did not cry after we got home, either. But it was traumatic enough that he has wanted nothing to do with swimming lessons since then.

Now he's eight years old, and we have been going to a pool frequently, and I could tell from his conversations that he wanted to try new things in the water. But while we were in the water, he didn't want me to teach or even to suggest. If I would say, "Try this," he would get frustrated or angry with me. One evening, recently, at bedtime, he was talking about how he could go as far as four feet, but he couldn't go as far as five feet deep because he wasn't tall enough. I said, "You know how to float, so it really makes no difference how deep the water is." He got upset with me and replied, "It does too. I'm just not tall enough." Then he declared, "I never want to take swimming lessons," and started crying. Fortunately, I was in a frame of mind where I could be relatively objective, but still supportive, and I said something about how the idea of swimming lessons really frightened him because of that experience he had had at the age of five. He talked about it and cried about it, saying that he had really been scared, and that he didn't want to do that again. He cried for a total of 15 or 20 minutes about that episode.

The next day, we went swimming again, and he said, "Mom, can I go where it's five feet deep?" For the first time, he wanted to go in deep water over his head, and he did! In fact, he enjoyed it so much, he didn't want to get out of the water! Then, the next time we went swimming after that, he started to jump in and dive for pennies and kiss the bottom of the pool!

In the case of conditioned fears, emotional discharge can also be helpful. These fears would not develop if the child had enough opportunities to cry with somebody's aware attention.

A good guideline is to allow and encourage emotional discharge as much as possible after your child has been frightened
for any reason. Sometimes a child will not cry easily. This could
be because she is not feeling safe enough. The frightening event
must be no longer threatening, and the child must feel a certain
amount of safety and security before she will be able to cry. As
long as she feels that danger is still lurking, a full release of
feelings cannot occur.

Children take active steps to heal themselves of their fears, and
this is done primarily through their play and laughter. They
actually set up therapeutic situations for themselves if allowed
enough time for free play. Since I live in Southern California, I
have had many opportunities to observe young children at the
beach. The ocean must seem to a young child an immensely
powerful and unpredictable force. Children often run a little way
into the water, getting their feet wet, but, as a wave approaches,
they quickly run out again to avoid being hit by the wave. This
activity is almost always accompanied by peals of laughter. As
some of their fear becomes dissipated by repetitions of this game,
they gradually venture further and further into the water. They
make sure that they keep a good balance between fear and safety
by not going in too far, but also by not staying too far away.

A casual adult observer may think that such games at the beach
are mere child's play of little importance, not realizing that the
children are engaged in determined and calculated efforts to help
themselves conquer their fears of the ocean. Whenever children's
games involve hearty laughter, there is probably an element of
fear that they are grappling with.

If children do not invent a game that promotes laughter about
their fears, parents can help them laugh in playful settings. It is
important that the child feel unthreatened in order for the
situation to be therapeutic, but it is also necessary for the child to
be exposed to the feared element, at least partially or symbolically. The child's attention must be both on the distress and on
the safety of the present moment, otherwise no laughter will
occur (Rothbart, 1973). This feeling of simultaneous distress and

safety has been called "the balance of attention" (Jackins, 1970) or "the distancing of emotion" (Scheff, 1979). It is always a necessary requirement before any therapeutic emotional release (in the form of laughter or crying) can occur. If a child is too overwhelmed by his fear, ("underdistanced") he will not be able to laugh or cry. Likewise, if the feared element is not present at all ("overdistanced") he will not feel at all frightened, and also will not laugh or cry (Scheff, 1979).

You can experiment in order to find the most effective way of bringing up your child's fear, while maintaining an atmosphere of fun and safety. This kind of play therapy is further discussed in Chapter 4. The following example illustrates how I used laughter therapy to help my daughter deal with a fear of toilets:

> At three years of age, Sarah was still reluctant to use the toilet because of a fear of falling in. On several occasions, I brought a stuffed animal with us to the bathroom, and made it act as though *it* was terrified of the toilet. This always brought hearty laughter from my daughter. She was usually able to relax and use the toilet after these games, and gradually her fear subsided and she became willing to use the toilet by herself.

In many cases, both accurate information *and* a release of feelings are necessary in order for a child to overcome fears. Usually, when a child does something scary, this provides her not only with an opportunity to release tensions by laughing but also with new, correct information about reality. Children wading into the ocean while laughing are gaining information about the force of the waves compared to their own strength. They acquire this knowledge while discharging their fears.

Children are often attracted to and fascinated by the very objects they fear the most. This attraction probably stems from the urge all children have to overcome their fears. They know intuitively that they are going to have to experience their fear in order to overcome it. They are also interested in acquiring as much information as they can about the object. But at the same time their fear makes them keep at a safe distance. These two opposing tendencies result in an interesting approach/avoidance phenomenon:

> A three-year-old boy was terrified of snakes. He imagined them crawling around him in the dark. When shown a large, snake-like worm one day at a museum, he was fascinated by it, but he kept a safe distance away and wanted his mother to hold him.

A previous section mentioned the experiment done with little Albert, who developed a conditioned fear of rats because of their association with a loud, frightening noise. In order to cure little Albert of his fear of rats, he would need both new, correct information, and an opportunity to discharge his feelings. Behavioral psychologists have focused almost exclusively on providing information. This could be accomplished by showing Albert a rat repeatedly without the accompanying noise, so that he can learn that the association does not always occur. This procedure is called "extinction," and behaviorists have known for a long time that conditioning can be undone in this manner. However, little Albert would most certainly cry or laugh while being shown a rat, and this emotional release would allow the extinction process to work thoroughly and effectively. He has experienced a hurtful, frightening event, and this fear and pain must be expressed. Without the discharge, extinction would not be complete or permanent.

To conclude, children cannot overcome their fears by avoiding what is frightening, nor will they become brave by being told not to be afraid. They must fully experience their fear, sometimes by doing what is scary (at least partially or symbolically), while at the same time feeling safe. Part of their attention must be on their fear, but they also need to be aware of the unthreatening reality of the present moment. When this balance of attention is achieved, then emotional release in the form of laughter (and sometimes crying and shaking) will flow spontaneously, and the children will heal themselves of their fears.

What About Fears of Unknown Origin?

With symbolic fears of unknown origin, such as a fear of monsters under the bed, the parents' job is considerably more challenging. If you suspect an underlying reason, such as anxiety caused by a new sibling or other distressing life experiences, you can try to encourage the child to express her feelings about the real problem. If no cause can be discerned, then you can work with whatever symbol is the focus of the fears.

In these cases, information is helpful but often insufficient. When my daughter developed a fear of crocodiles at five years of age, she said: "I know there aren't any crocodiles in my room, because they need to live in water, but I am still scared." With these fears, the guidelines of encouraging both laughter and crying are still beneficial:

> Sarah's fear of crocodiles was so great at one point that she was afraid to be alone in her room or even to go to the bathroom alone. Her fear had become more and more intense, but without any crying or laughter occurring. I decided that she needed help, so I got out a crocodile puppet one evening, and told her it was a baby crocodile that needed to be taken care of. I kept her laughing heartily for 10 or 15 minutes. Later on, after the puppet was put away, she cried freely and heavily for 20 minutes about her fears while I stayed with her.

In this example, the puppet helped my daughter to lighten up enough so that she could laugh and cry about her fears. Until then, she had been locked in her fear so intensely that she could not release her feelings. They were too overwhelming (an example of "underdistancing"). My playful approach with a toy helped her to gain a new perspective and to feel safe enough to laugh and cry. With intense fears, many sessions like these may be needed before the fears will subside completely. Another playful approach that may help the child laugh is to let the child play the role of the feared animal or monster while the parent pretends to be frightened.

Many fears are ultimately rooted in a fear of death. Any time children play games that bring hearty laughter, there is some fear being released. Parents can help children overcome a fear of death by encouraging such games.

There is a popular singing game for preschool-aged children called "Ring around the Rosie." It is believed by some that this song originated during the Middle Ages following a bubonic plague epidemic in London. There are many versions, but one old version (from *The Real Mother Goose,* Rand McNally & Co., 1916) goes as follows:

Ring a ring o'roses,
A pocketful of posies.
Tisha! Tisha!
We all fall down!

The third line could have been an imitation of sneezing, one of the first signs of bubonic plague, and the last line could have been a referral to dropping dead. (During this line, all of the singers typically fall down.) This song must have been quite therapeutic for those children who survived the plague, but who saw hundreds of their friends and relatives die. It provided them with the much needed tension release mechanism of laughter.

Today, children who know nothing of the plague laugh, sometimes hysterically, at the end of the song when everyone falls down. Could they be dealing with their fear of death through laughter? It seems likely. Falling down is certainly similar to dying. One reason this song has survived throughout the ages is probably the fact that it provides therapeutic laughter.

Fear of death is almost universal in both children and adults. This is one reason that amusement parks (such as Disneyland and Disneyworld) are so popular. Almost every attraction at these places has an element of fear in it, whether it is a thrilling roller coaster ride, a jungle cruise with alligators popping out of the water, or a haunted house with life-sized ghosts. Children (and adults) laugh in these situations because fears are brought up in a safe context. After a full day of such laughter, they go home more relaxed and slightly less afraid of their own mortality. It is not surprising that people wish to return to these amusement parks again and again.

What Causes Nightmares and Night Terrors?

Nightmares are caused by fears of any origin. Recurring nightmares may have their origin in very early trauma, such as a distressing birth experience (Janov, 1983). Any recent frightening or confusing event can also cause nightmares. When children have enough opportunities to cry about distressing events during the day, nightmares are less likely to occur.

If your child has a nightmare, you can ask him to talk about it and let him cry as needed. If he is too scared to talk about it, you can try to lighten things up and get him to laugh. After some laughter, he may be ready to tell his dream and perhaps even cry about it.

Sometimes a young child will wake up at night screaming, and not seem to be aware of his surroundings. He will yell out words and phrases that make little sense, as if he were experiencing a nightmare. In addition to loud crying, these night terrors can be accompanied by angry movements and sometimes even trembling and shaking. It can take as little as a few minutes, or as long as an hour, before the child seems to be back in touch with reality and is able to respond normally. The child usually awakens in the morning happy and relaxed, with no memory of the episode.

Unlike regular nightmares, that occur during REM (rapid eye movement) sleep, night terrors occur during deep sleep (also called Delta sleep). Night terrors can be frightening to parents. It may seem as if your child is "going crazy" or totally "out of control." You may find yourself agonizing over the fact that your child does not seem to see or hear you, and feel helpless in your attempts to gain his attention.

Night terrors are nothing to become alarmed about, because, just as with ordinary crying, they represent a healthy release and healing process. Any shaking that occurs is the release of heavy fears. The intensity of these nighttime crying sessions results from the fact that raw feelings are being expressed without any of the inhibitions normally present during waking hours. (In children who are encouraged to cry and rage, however, the intensity of night terrors is not likely to be any greater than the intensity of daytime crying.)

Night terrors can be triggered by a need to urinate or by a sudden noise or jolt. They are also more likely if there is unusual stress in a child's life, a new fear, or if there has been insufficient crying and raging during the day. But they can occur with no apparent cause at all, even though the child is allowed to cry openly during the day. Some children have them frequently, while others never experience them at all. You can be helpful by holding your child, speaking to him reassuringly, and waiting for the terror to pass. When he is done crying, he may drift peacefully off to sleep, or he may awaken and interact normally before going back to sleep.

What About Separation Anxiety Past the Age of Two?

Many young children are strongly attached to their mothers and other primary caretakers and do not like to be separated from them. Parents often wonder whether this is normal, and how long this behavior will continue.

Separation anxiety is still very common and normal in two-year-olds (Bowlby, 1973) and is nothing to be concerned about. Even older children cannot be expected to jump into strangers' arms or to be immediately happy when left with strangers. There is a strong tendency for children to prefer familiar people and familiar surroundings, and children will normally protest when left in an unfamiliar situation. This tendency must have had survival value in prehistoric times when hunter-gatherer groups needed to stay together. It also reflects the basic need of all children for continuity in caretakers.

When left with *familiar* and caring people, however, separation anxiety is normally not as evident as it was during the first two years. If a child is over two-and-a-half years of age and still has a strong separation anxiety when left with familiar people, this may be an indication of some kind of distress associated with separation other than the normal separation anxiety seen during infancy. Children this age possess enough language skills to understand that their parent is not leaving forever, and have the ability to visualize the parent's return. The distress they experience cannot therefore be attributed to an inability to understand the temporary nature of the separation.

There are several reasons that can cause a child to cry when her parents leave. One of these is simply a need to cry. Perhaps she does not cry freely with her parents because of their failure to accept crying. If the child is allowed to be with someone who is more accepting of her crying, she will then do the crying she needs to do. Sometimes parents, in spite of good intentions, come to act as control patterns for their children, especially if they have tended to use nursing, rocking, or entertainment as distracters when the child really needed to release feelings by crying. These children will seem to "need" the constant presence of their fathers or mothers just as some children become attached to stuffed toys, blankets, or a pacifier. These attachments are used as crutches to hold feelings in when crying has not been totally accepted and encouraged. When a separation from the parent occurs, it looks as if the child is crying about the separation itself, but in reality she may simply be discharging accumulated feelings from daily hurts and frustrations.

A second reason for crying when away from the parents is the possibility that the separation itself reminds the child of an earlier separation that *was* a new hurt because it occurred during infancy when the baby needed to have continuous and consistent care and could not understand that her parents would ever return. The child will make use of any new separation to attempt to cry about the earlier separation. If allowed to do so, the child will continue to cry each time the mother or father leaves, until she has completely healed herself of the effects of the early trauma. Being placed in an incubator at birth (or being separated from the parents right after birth for other reasons) may be the original separation that is triggered by later ones.

If you think that either of these reasons might account for your child's resistance to separation, then your child will benefit by being left and allowed to cry, provided the person you leave her with is someone she knows well and who is supportive and understanding of the crying. With that precaution, you will be sure that she is not suffering a new frightening experience, but merely healing herself from past traumas.

If your child has been quite happy with a certain caretaker, but then, one day, suddenly resists being left with that person, it is possible that she has been hurt or frightened while with the person. It can be something as innocuous as a new dog in the caretaker's home, or as serious as being hit or sexually abused. Children need to be trusted, and a sudden resistance to being with someone should be taken seriously and checked into.

There are other possible reasons for a reluctance to go to daycare or nursery school. Perhaps the child has been hit, teased, or rejected by another child. If your child has suffered a distressing experience such as this, and then refuses to go to school, you can help her express her feelings at home by role playing the incident and encouraging laughter. Depending on the age of your child, you may want to leave her at school, even though she protests, and allow her to cry there. This will be helpful only if there is an aware adult who is able to be lovingly supportive of her need to cry. For some children, especially very young ones, attending a nursery school with aggressive children may be too overwhelming. In this case, it makes little sense to force a child to stay against her will. In another six months or a year she may be ready to handle the situation better.

Another reason for unusual crying when a parent leaves is the possibility that the parent has been less attentive than usual. This can cause the child to have feelings of hurt and anger. Perhaps there has been a recent separation that was frightening to the child, such as the mother being hospitalized, or perhaps the parents are preoccupied with marital problems and have less attention than usual for the child. Any time a child needs to release feelings about the parents themselves, she will be more likely to save her crying for times that she is separated from them.

If you are not sure of the reason for your child's resistance to separation, or are not sure about how to deal with it, then trust your own feelings and inclinations. If it does not feel right to leave your child, then don't do so, even though other people may accuse you of "spoiling" your child or being "overprotective." Your own intuition is probably correct. Furthermore, your course of action must make sense to you and be a decision you can live with. If you discover later that you have misjudged a situation with your child, you can always try a different approach another day.

I would like to stress once again the importance of allowing young children time to become familiar with new situations before leaving them. There are huge individual differences in children. Some require more time than others to feel safe in new situations, and they need patience and understanding. A mother I interviewed expressed how difficult this was for her:

> I basically have this idea that a four-year-old ought to be independent and outgoing, but she's not always like that. I really get uncomfortable when we go some place and she hangs back and climbs in my arms or hides behind me. That drives me nuts. I feel like I'm being sucked into this mire of having to do something I'm not in the mood for doing at the moment, like comforting and holding her. Because it's not in my plans, I have very little patience with it. I want her to separate and go off and be happy. But the day at nursery school when she did separate easily from me, I went home and cried!

Even though children may handle short separations quite well, it is best not to impose long separations between children and their parents (or primary caretakers). Two-year-olds should not be away from their parents for more than ten days, and three- to five-year-olds should not be separated for more than three weeks. Six- to nine-year-olds can tolerate a separation of up to four weeks. Separations that are longer than these recommended lengths can interfere with the parent/child bond and cause potential harm (Magid & McKelvey, 1987).

Exercises

Explore your childhood.

1. List the fears you remember having as a child. How were these dealt with by your parents?

2. Do you remember a nightmare you had as a child? Talk about it.

3. Were you ever teased for being scared? How did it make you feel?

Express your feelings about your child.

1. Make a list of your child's current fears and try to figure out where they came from.

2. How do you feel about your child's fears?

3. Do you have any fears about your child's safety or well-being? What are they? Talk about them.

Nurture yourself.

1. Join a therapy or support group that encourages you to laugh.

2. Do you currently have any fears or phobias? Pick one of them and take steps to overcome it (on your own, or with the help of counseling or therapy).

3. See a funny movie or show, or get together with friends that make you laugh.

CHAPTER 3: LIVING AND LEARNING

This chapter discusses the acquisition of new information through the senses, which is the first important step in learning. Children take in new facts continuously, just by living and experiencing the world. They learn by direct, concrete experiences, by observing and listening, by asking questions, through books, and through television. Some of these sources of information are helpful and pleasurable, while others cause confusion or anxiety. In some cases the child is actively involved in seeking new information, while in others the child is a passive recipient. The second half of the learning process is accomplished through children's play. This is discussed in Chapter 4.

What Kinds of Concrete Experiences Are Beneficial For Young Children?

People of all ages learn through direct experiences, but this is especially true for young children. This is by far the most effective source of new information for them. Most cities offer zoos, museums, libraries, parks, and an occasional circus or fair. Although artificial entertainment can be fun and educational, simpler activities that are closer to nature (and usually also cheaper as well) can provide rich and varied learning experiences. Wading in a real creek with live frogs and mossy rocks will provide more varied learning experiences for your child than wading in an artificial, concrete wading pool.

If you live in a big city and cannot easily reach a natural setting, do not despair, because cities offer many learning opportunities for young children. Assuming you have already taken your child to the zoo, library, museums, and parks, where else can you go? The possibilities are endless. You can visit the train station or airport. Take your child to see the newborn babies at the maternity ward of a hospital. Attend the rehearsal of a concert or play. Visit the city dump to see what happens to the garbage. Go to the newspaper printer and ask if you can watch the presses running. Perhaps you can visit a bakery, a construction site, a university laboratory, or a factory.

If you have opportunities to travel, you can take your child to mountains, rivers, lakes, forests, deserts, and farms, and you can visit other cities. Young children are eager and ready to see and experience the world. They want to learn about real life, about what grown-ups do, where things come from, and where they go. The more they can see of the real world, the better they will understand it and figure out their own role in it.

As you expose your child to varied experiences be sure to allow enough time for her to assimilate the information, in order to avoid overstimulation. Children need to talk about their experiences, ask questions, and re-enact them through play.

How Can I Share My Own Interests With My Child?

Everybody needs to engage in creative activities, develop new skills, and acquire new information. This holds true at all ages. Parents sometimes wonder how to pursue their own activities and often feel guilty for taking time away from their children to do so.

Many hobbies and interests can be pursued at home when children are present, and the children benefit immensely by seeing their parents involved in creative and stimulating activities. Although you are not giving direct attention to your children when you pursue your own hobby or interest at home, you are nevertheless giving them a valuable learning experience.

One way that children can learn from their parents' activities is by being allowed to participate in some way. If you enjoy gardening, perhaps your children can help dig, plant seeds, and pull weeds. If your hobby is baking bread, children can help by measuring, pouring, and mixing ingredients. If you are a stamp collector, your children can help sort the stamps.

There is an additional, indirect benefit for children when their parents pursue hobbies and interests. This is the information children acquire about the learning process. It is important for children to see adults engaged in the process of learning. When children see only the result of learning and practice, such as a polished concert, they may acquire an unrealistic and distorted picture of the learning process. However, when they have opportunities to observe an entire project from conception to finished product, they learn that mistakes are an integral part of learning, even for adults. They also realize that determination and perseverance are necessary in order to master a new skill or to create something (Holt, 1981).

It is important that parents refrain from beginning a new hobby or activity with the sole purpose of teaching their children, because the children might sense the fakeness of the situation and resent the attempts at instruction. Children need to see adults doing meaningful things, at times, which are not artificially contrived activities for the benefit of the children. Here is an example:

> I had once expressed an interest in learning to play the accordeon, so I was not too surprised when my husband gave me a second-hand accordeon as a present. I had never played one, but was determined to learn. With the help of a music book, I taught myself how to play and eventually became proficient enough to accompany many folk songs. My children watched me practice, heard my mistakes, and witnessed my perseverance. When my husband brought home a second-hand trumpet, Nicky (age 9) decided that he would learn to play it, and proceeded to do so (with the help of after-school lessons). A small guitar was given to Sarah for her sixth birthday, and she too had no doubts that she could learn to play it. I showed her a few chords and she soon accompanied herself singing simple songs. I think that my children's confidence stemmed partly

from having observed me learn to play a musical instrument. It is interesting that my accordeon playing was something done entirely for my own pleasure. I had no intention of teaching my children anything or of being a model for them to emulate. (In fact, I sometimes felt guilty about not spending that time with them!) It was only later that I realized the positive effect this had on them.

Should Young Children Be Exposed to Violence?

Violence is one aspect of reality from which young children should be protected. However, this is not the attitude of our culture. It is felt by many producers of children's television programs that it is perfectly fine to expose children to scenes of violence and killing. Young children can become quite frightened by observing violence, whether in real life or on television. Violence is not an activity that is inherently human, but rather a result of distress. Human beings would not hurt each other unless they themselves had been hurt as children and not allowed to express their hurt feelings. For this reason, exposure to violence can result not only in anxiety but in misinformation as well.

Children need a foundation on which to build a positive concept about human nature. They need to have a certain number of good experiences, be treated with gentleness, love, and respect, and see others treated that way. Once they have established faith in the goodness of humanity, they can then be told gradually about violence and war. They do need to learn about these things eventually, because violence is an undeniable part of the world. When you begin to expose your children to information about war, it is important to balance it with information about peace efforts and explanations of why people try to hurt each other. This will help prevent them from feeling overwhelmed, frightened, or discouraged.

How Can I Answer My Child's Questions About Death?

Death is a very uncomfortable subject for many people, and few parents are able or willing to discuss it openly. This is because

many of us have unresolved fears about death. Also, we may wish
to protect our children from knowing about such things. The word
"death" itself is almost taboo in our culture. Instead, we talk
about "putting the dog to sleep," or about the grandmother who
"passed away."

Children do not have these inhibitions about death, and their
questions and curiosity reflect an eagerness and interest to learn
as much about death as they can. The directness of children's
questions can be shocking to parents: "When are you going to
die?" "Will I die?" "Why do people die?" "What can dead people
do?" "Do worms eat dead people?"

Children need accurate and concrete information about death,
and they deserve to have their questions answered as directly and
completely as possible, even though we may feel that death is not
a subject meriting casual discussion. Here is what a mother said
to me about her feelings when her son began to ask questions
about death:

> As soon as Gary could talk and ask questions, around the age of
> two-and-a-half, he began to ask questions about death. He was
> fascinated by dead animals, dead birds, anything. I didn't know
> how much information to give him, and I was really upset and
> perplexed about it. I didn't want him to know about all that
> stuff, and I tried to shield him from it. My concern was that it
> was awfully morbid, so I would try to change the subject,
> because his questions were so specific. Then I realized that it
> was my problem, not his. After that, it became easier for me. I
> realized that I needed to answer his questions as directly as
> possible and to give him as much information as I could. I got to
> the point where I could really enjoy telling him about the
> maggots eating the body of the birds, and dead people too, and
> what graveyards were for. He wanted to know all the tech-
> nicalities about disintegrating bodies, how long it takes, and so
> on. It was one of his earliest preoccupations. He just had to get
> all that information. Now he's five years old, and he doesn't ask
> questions like that any more, because he's got that information.

A good way for children to learn about death is by seeing dead
plants and animals. You can casually point out dead flies, snails,

flowers, and trees, or else wait until your child notices them. Small pets, such as fish or mice, provide excellent opportunities to learn about death because they do not usually live very long. Do not be surprised if, after a burial of a pet, your child expresses a desire to dig up the animal and look at it! This is his way of gaining valuable information about death and decomposition.

Some children develop misconceptions about death, and these need to be clarified. A common idea is that it hurts to be dead. Children need to know that people no longer feel pain when they are dead. Another confusion concerns death and sleep, and it is important to make a clear distinction between the two. Instead of telling your child about "putting a dog to sleep" (so that it would no longer suffer), it is best to say directly that the dog was killed or "made dead," and to explain how it was done and why. Otherwise, the child may develop a fear of falling asleep, thinking he will never wake up again, just like the dog.

If a family member or friend has died, concrete information is best. When a child is told that his grandfather "went to heaven" this will not help him understand what has really happened. The child needs to know that grandfather is dead and that he can no longer do anything. If religious explanations of death are offered, these need to be given with the awareness that such explanations can be easily distorted by young children into frightening concepts that have little to do with religion (Furman, 1986).

When a child asks a parent, "Are you going to die?" this may reflect a fear of being rejected or abandoned. A good way to answer this might be, "Everybody dies eventually, but I don't expect to die for a long, long time." It is also helpful to discuss with young children alternative caretaking arrangements and to let them know who would take care of them if their parents should die. This may be reassuring to a child who seems to be preoccupied by the possibility of his parents' death.

How Can I Give My Child Information About Sexuality?

Most children can distinguish between males and females by three years of age (Kreitler and Kreitler, 1965). This is also the age at which children typically begin to ask questions about genital differences and reproduction (Selzer, 1974).

The best way to give children information about sexuality and reproduction is simply to answer their questions. The following recommended guidelines are from a researcher who studied early childhood sex education (Koblinsky et al., 1986). Although geared for early childhood educators, these guidelines are also useful for parents. Before answering a question, you can find out from your child how much he already knows, so you will know where to begin. It is important to use correct vocabulary in describing genitals and reproductive organs, and to give accurate information. The use of books can be helpful, but avoid using plants and animals as substitutes for discussing human reproduction. This can be a source of confusion, since young children may have difficulty generalizing from plants and animals to human beings. Providing natural opportunities for children to observe each other is a good way for them to learn about genital differences.

When a child asks a question, it is best to answer the specific question without offering more information than is requested. When a little girl sees a boy's penis for the first time and asks "What's that?", there is no need to offer an extensive explanation of sexuality and reproduction. The child may be interested only in genital differences at the moment, and not be ready for information about sexual intercourse. You can simply say, "That's a penis. All boys have penises."

Many families and hospitals are now allowing young children to be present at the birth of a sibling (Simkin, 1987). Aside from providing a way for siblings to bond to each other right from the start, this is an excellent way of helping children learn where babies come from. There is nothing inherently traumatic in observing a birth, but young children do need to be carefully prepared for such an event. Guidelines for doing this are discussed in Chapter 6.

Many parents wonder if it is traumatic for young children to see their parents engaged in sexual intercourse. This is a concern especially for parents who let their children sleep in the same room. In the American culture, perhaps because of the puritanical influence of the early pioneers, it is considered inappropriate to let young children observe adults engaged in sexual activities, or even to see a film containing sexual scenes. It is ironic that our culture shields children from scenes of human love-making but ruthlessly exposes them to scenes of human killing. There are many cultures in which sexuality is not hidden from children, with no observable ill effects. An example of such a culture is the traditional !Kung culture of Africa (Shostak, 1983).

Although the psychoanalytic literature is full of examples of children being traumatized by inadvertently observing their parents engaging in sexual intercourse, it is quite likely that the trauma stems, not from observing the act itself, but from the parents' *reaction* to the child's sudden and unexpected entry into their room. Any anger directed at the child (although understandable from the adult's point of view) is likely to be a cause of anxiety and guilt in the child, who may then come to associate these painful feelings with sexuality itself.

If your child should happen to see you making love there is no need to become overly concerned. Try to remain calm and to answer her questions in a matter-of-fact manner. Although you may be irritated, try not to make her feel guilty for interrupting your love-making.

How Can I Minimize the Effect of Sexism on My Child?

We live in a sexist culture. More and more people are becoming aware of this, and recognizing the importance of raising children in ways that do not mold them into stereotypes of "male" and "female." These stereotypes are hurtful to children, because they limit what the children can feel and do, thereby preventing them from developing their full human potential.

The cultural message is that boys are smarter and more capable than girls, and that girls' primary role in life is to become mothers. Many of the ways that parents, relatives, friends, and teachers treat children are ultimately based on these two underlying sexist assumptions (Pogrebin, 1980).

Before the age of two years, children do not typically show much sex-typed preference or awareness, but by three years of age, children have learned which toys are culturally acceptable for each sex to play with, and which clothing, tools, and activities go with adult males or females (Vener & Snyder, 1966). It is not long before the children themselves enforce these norms with each other. A study done in nursery schools found that boys who played with dolls, dress-up clothes, kitchen toys, or art materials were criticized by their classmates six times more often than other children (Fagot, 1977).

Some people claim that boys are inherently different from girls and that preferences and sex roles in society are caused entirely by these genetic differences. It is a fact that boys are generally more aggressive than girls, engage in more rough-and-tumble play, and play more with transportation toys, woodworking materials, and blocks. Girls, on the other hand, typically engage in more doll play, domestic play, art activities, dress-up, and dancing (Fagot & Kronsberg, 1982). However, these observed differences do not necessarily mean that the reason for them is biological. Boys and girls could choose these activities simply because parents treat them differently and have different expectations for them.

It has been shown that parents tend to treat boys and girls differently, sometimes without realizing it, from the day they are born. Mothers typically spend more time talking to their newborn daughters than to sons, but they rock, touch, and hold their sons more than their daughters. These differences in parents' behavior towards newborns was observed to occur even though the behavior of newborn boys and girls is the same. As children grow past the toddler stage, parents continue to treat boys differently from girls. Parents tend to buy more dolls and domestic toys for their daughters and more transportation toys and sports equipment for their sons. Parents also continue to interact with daughters more verbally and with sons more physically (Fagot & Kronsberg,

1982). Girls are socialized for dependency: they are encouraged to touch and stay close to their mothers and are taught to be pretty and clean. Boys are expected to be independent and tough, and to keep their feelings to themselves, especially emotions such as tenderness, fear, compassion, and sadness. Girls are allowed to express a broader range of emotions. Boys are also disciplined differently from girls. One study found that parents spank their sons three times more often than they spank their daughters (Straus, 1971).

If you wish to take steps towards treating your children in less stereotyped ways, a good way to begin is with the kinds of toys you give them. This means giving dolls to both sexes, as well as toy trucks and trains. Parents also need to become aware of their attitudes towards their children's play. It does little good to give dolls to boys, but then to ignore them when they play with the dolls. If you give them dolls, you need to encourage doll play just as you would with a girl, and provide them with the accessories as well (such as doll beds, clothing, and dishes).

This is more difficult than it might seem, because there are several factors that can intervene. Friends and relatives might not be as enlightened as you are, and may tend to give the more traditional, sex-stereotyped toys. You can help create a better balance by compensating for any toys not received. If your daughter receives only dolls from relatives, you yourself can give her a tool kit for her birthday.

A fear of homosexuality ("homophobia") can interfere with parents' good intentions. In our culture, heterosexuality in men has been closely linked with the idea of being tough, aggressive, and unfeeling. A "real man" is considered to be one who does not display nurturing behavior. Because of this unfortunate attitude, many parents actually feel that to encourage the "softer," nurturing feelings and behavior in their sons would make them homosexual. It has been shown that homosexuality cannot be reliably predicted from childhood behavior (Simon & Gagnon, 1976), and that sexual attraction has little to do with either gender identity or gender-role behavior (Green, 1976). It is not known what makes people become homosexuals, but it is clear that non-sexist child-rearing is *not* one of the factors.

It is important to encourage your child to have friends of both sexes. There is nothing to worry about if your son plays with girls or your daughter plays with boys. After the age of four or five, boys are sometimes considered to be "sissies" if they play with girls, but during adolescence, parents become worried if their sons fail to show an interest in girls. Boys are expected to develop meaningful relationships with girls after having been deprived of friendships with girls during childhood. This does not make sense. The best way for the two sexes to develop good relationships with each other is by playing together from early childhood on. As a parent, you can suggest that your children invite both boys and girls to their birthday parties, and you can work towards the development of sports teams, clubs, and other activities in your community that include children of both sexes.

Segregating the sexes during childhood will not protect children from becoming homosexuals. In fact, the opposite may be true. It is well known that homosexual experimentation abounds in all-male sports teams and private all-boy and all-girl schools, the very places that are supposed to turn little boys into "real men," and little girls into "ladies" (Pogrebin, 1980).

Many children's books are sexist. Books about animals often use only the male pronouns, as if female animals did not even exist. Often the only female animals in books are those that are obviously mothers. Male and female characters usually have traditional sex-roles, with the males having the most adventures and taking the most initiative and risks, while the females are passive and domestic. Most television programs are no better than books, and have more of an impact because of the vivid visual portrayal on the screen.

You can counteract these influences in the home by changing male pronouns to female ones as you read to your children, and finding children's books that are non-sexist. It is also helpful to limit television viewing and to discuss sexist stereotypes and attitudes.

Children are influenced by all the factors I have discussed, but the most important information you can give your children comes from your own model and example. Parents who limit their behavior to conform to sexist stereotypes cannot expect their children to grow up realizing their full potential. Children learn much more from observing you than from any toys or books you may give them. Here is my own experience:

> When Sarah was three years old, one of her toy trucks was broken, and she showed it to me and said, "Papa will fix it." I felt insulted, because she had not even considered the fact that I might be able to fix it. I then realized that I had usually left the repairs around the home to my husband, even though I was perfectly capable of learning to repair things myself. So I took my daughter's truck and fixed it!

It is also important to allow children of both sexes to feel and express feelings of all kinds. Our culture encourages girls to be fearful and boys to be aggressive, but boys have just as many fears as girls, and girls experience just as much anger as boys. It has been observed that boys in child-guidance clinics have usually been referred for aggressive, destructive, and competitive behavior, whereas girls are referred for problems involving fears, shyness, and lack of self-confidence (Chesler, 1971). This is a direct result of sexist child-rearing. I have already mentioned that boys are usually stopped from crying more than girls are, and taught to repress their feelings more in general. As adults, it is not surprising that, after years of keeping their feelings in check, many men tend to explode suddenly and with little provocation. They tend to become angry and violent because they have had no other acceptable outlet for their feelings (Yachnes, 1973).

It is not unusual for children to go through a stage of conforming to the sex-role stereotypes. Little boys may say they are not interested in dolls, in spite of being given them, and little girls may show great preference for dolls over toy trucks and trains. There seems to be a need for children to experience fully the sex roles that society dictates, in spite of a non-sexist home environment.

Children probably feel the need to adopt traditional male or female behavior in order to be accepted by their peers.

Even though your efforts may appear to be in vain when your children are young and easily influenced by their peers, it is important to continue providing non-sexist influences at home. The positive effects may not appear until adulthood, when the grown-up child will feel free to consider a wide range of career options, unhampered by sexist stereotypes.

It is clear that sexism hurts boys just as much as it hurts girls and deprives everyone of full humanness. Anything that can be done in the home to counteract these influences will benefit not only the children themselves but ultimately the entire world.

How Can I Help My Child Develop Intellectual Abilities and New Skills?

Parents naturally want to provide an environment that allows their children to develop the ability to think and learn well. Research has shown that parents can have considerable influence on their children's intellectual development. The home environment can play a crucial role in helping young children reach their highest potential.

Parental warmth and nurturance have been found to lead to increased intellectual competence in children (Bayley & Schaefer, 1964). It is not surprising why this is so. Children who feel secure and loved will be more likely to explore their environment and have more attention for thinking and learning, because their efforts will not be directed continuously towards trying to fill their basic emotional needs.

Parental discipline techniques have also been found to affect children's intellectual abilities. Intellectual development is hindered by the use of authoritarian child-rearing methods and punishment (Baumrind, 1971). On the other hand, children's thinking skills are enhanced when parents use discipline techniques that appeal to a sense of reason, such as offering explanations for restrictions (Radin, 1970).

It is a common belief that the use of praise is a good way to encourage learning and help children feel confident about their abilities. Surprisingly, however, some forms of praise can have the reverse effect of what is intended, leading to overdependence on others for approval and lowered self-confidence. Praise can also discourage effort and be perceived by the child as a form of manipulation (Hitz & Driscoll, 1988). Rather than offer value judgments about a child's performance ("That was very good"), parents can be more helpful by providing encouragement and focusing on the process and the child's feelings rather than on the product. Giving specific feedback about a child's performance (without value judgments) allows children to see their own progress, but avoids comparing them to each other.

When a child accomplishes something new, such as putting a puzzle together, you can simply say enthusiastically, "You did it!" or "I bet you're proud of yourself!" or "That's the hardest puzzle you've ever done." If your child proudly shows you a drawing, you can ask her to tell you about it and then listen respectfully, or you can notice the different colors she used, or describe how it makes you feel ("That reminds me of a hot summer day"). Children need to have their accomplishments acknowledged but they do not benefit from having them judged.

The presence of stimulating materials in the home is another important factor in intellectual development. It has been found that children who come from stimulating home environments score higher on tests of mental abilities than children whose homes lack stimulation (Bradley & Caldwell, 1976).

Young children become frequently frustrated in their attempts to learn new skills. These frustrations must be dealt with before meaningful learning or thinking can occur. It is possible to prevent some frustrations by arranging situations that allow for maximum success rather than failure. If your child is helping you bake cookies, you can select a mixing bowl that does not tip over easily. A child learning to tie shoe laces may need extra long ones at first. Also, if a child is attempting to do something that is clearly too difficult for her, it is beneficial to offer help, simplify the task, or redirect her efforts towards a more realistic goal.

In spite of these precautions, there will be many mistakes and frustrations that are inevitable as children struggle to become competent and skilled human beings. When children become frustrated, they need patient understanding so they can vent their feelings, which will occur by crying and raging (as described in Chapter 1). This outlet is sometimes necessary before children can succeed at the task they are trying to accomplish. It does little good to try to stop the crying, because the frustration has *already* occurred and needs to be expressed.

A mother reported to me how crying helped her child master a frustrating learning situation:

> My daughter, age six-and-a-half, was having a difficult time playing two piano pieces by heart and keeping them separate. Finally, she just started crying and said she couldn't do it. I let her cry while holding her in my arms (for perhaps five minutes solid), and we hardly spoke at all. After crying, she wanted to try again, and she was able to keep the pieces separate! She never had a problem with them from that time on.

When painful feelings of frustration and failure are repressed, they can accumulate and lead to lowered self-confidence or an inability to think clearly in new learning situations. The following example describes a three-year-old boy's reluctance to try a new skill because of feelings that may have occurred during previous unsuccessful learning situations. His father described to me how he helped his son overcome these feelings:

> He claimed that he couldn't put his shirt on by himself, and began crying. I noticed that he was holding the shirt over his head without really trying to put it on. I was sure he could do it by himself, so I refrained from helping him, but offered encouragement for him to try. He cried hard for about 15 minutes and then easily put his shirt on! He was very proud of himself, and joyfully took it off and put it back on again several times to show off and practice his new skill.

The root of learning difficulties often resides in confusing and painful experiences that children have lived through, but without being able to express or resolve them (Weissglass & Weissglass, 1987). In extreme situations, some children have accumulated so much chronic distress that they lose their ability to concentrate or to attend to situations that require a mental effort. They "tune out" because their attention is too much preoccupied by their emotions. Children with this problem (called "Attention Deficit Disorder") have been helped with therapy that allows them to begin expressing their feelings (Oaklander, 1978).

Children who are allowed to express all their painful feelings openly have excellent learning and thinking abilities and may even astound others by their talents. Follow-up observations of children who completed therapy (involving a release of feelings with an empathic listener) have revealed a high ability to concentrate and excel in specific areas. These children were compared to others who began therapy but did not finish, and were found to be more well-rounded and competent in both academic and social skills (Emerson, 1989). When children are unhampered by distress, their brains and bodies are free to function at their maximum potential. We may eventually need to revise our concept of what constitutes normal or average abilities, because all children have the potential to become what is now considered "bright."

To conclude, in order to ensure optimal intellectual development, several factors should all be present from birth on: a warm, loving, and non-punitive environment, encouragement and acknowledgment of progress (without value judgments), appropriate stimulation, and an atmosphere that accepts crying and raging. If you have not been able to provide an optimal learning environment for your child, there is no need to be overly concerned, because it is never too late to begin making beneficial changes. The human brain is resilient, and children can and do recover from early distress or lack of stimulation.

What Kind of Books Are Best For Young Children and How Can I Help My Child Learn to Read?

Many parents are eager for their children to learn to read at an early age, but early reading is not necessarily beneficial for children, especially if they have been pushed to excel in this area. A better approach is to proceed indirectly and offer the kind of stimulation that will allow children to become motivated to read later on, when they are truly ready. There are several steps you can take to help your child develop a love of books and a positive attitude toward reading.

There is no doubt that reading to children helps them learn to enjoy books. It is also an effective way of developing children's imagination, sense of humor, thinking and memory skills, and it provides times of closeness and shared enjoyment. In a national survey done in the United States, it was found that the top students in first grade had had early reading experience. Before they started school, their parents had read to them, some almost every day (Jackson, 1977).

Picture books can be shown to infants, and, as children grow older, short story books can be introduced. It helps to select books that relate to the child's experiences and interests. For example, if you take your child on a boat, plane, or train ride, you can read her books about boats, planes, or trains, both before and after the trip. Although children can acquire new information through books, this can never substitute for real, concrete experiences.

Fairy tales are best saved until children are at least five years of age, because until that age they are busy trying to understand reality (Bettleheim,1975). Fairy tales, with their imaginary creatures, and symbolism of good and evil, can cause fear and confusion in very young children. Three-year-olds are still trying to learn which animals bite people and which do not. Reading to them about fantasy worlds containing trolls, enchanted birds, and unicorns will only confuse them. Simple, realistic stories are better for very young children.

There are many different kinds of books that can be shared with young children in addition to story books. Children can also enjoy books of art, poetry, music, science, jokes, and history. Activity and game books can be sources of much fun. If you and your child enjoy exploring the world of books together, your child will naturally want to learn to read. It is also important to give children opportunities to notice other uses for written language, such as correspondence, recipes, guide books, catalogs, games, and road signs.

Children will become more interested in learning to read if they see their parents enjoying reading. In the same survey mentioned earlier, it was found that children whose parents showed an interest in reading were good readers (Jackson, 1977). Let your child see you reading books, magazines, and newspapers. Children naturally want to imitate their parents.

There are many excellent educational games and activities for young children. These games can help children develop pre-reading skills. However, it is best not to force any activity or to turn a game into a structured teaching situation. If the children are having fun, it means they are learning something and their skills are being challenged. The goal of any activity with young children should be to have fun rather than try to teach.

Children can become bored, frustrated, or anxious when others attempt to teach them how to read before they are ready to learn, before they have requested to be taught, or in a manner that is not meaningful to their way of thinking. Some children are considered to be "learning disabled" if they do not read by the age of seven or eight. Although a small percentage of children do have neurological problems that make reading difficult for them, this label can be very harmful if misused, and can impair future learning, thereby becoming a self-fulfilling prophecy (Armstrong, 1987). Late readers often have other interests at first, but, when they finally learn to read, do so quickly and effortlessly and enjoy reading immensely.

What Kind of School Is Best For Young Children?

The best kind of school for young children is one in which free play is allowed most of the time. Children under eight years of age are usually not ready for formal, structured teaching, or sitting still for long periods of time. Attempts to impose this on them may result in resentment, frustration, confusion, boredom, loss of interest in learning, or loss of inner directedness.

Children who have been well loved and who have had opportunities to heal themselves of past hurts (as described in Chapter 1) will spontaneously direct their own learning. They will acquire information and skills, provided they are given the freedom and resources needed to do so.

When a child asks to be taught something, it is important to teach him in whatever manner he wants to be taught, whether it be giving information, correcting the child in some way, or quizzing him. Unasked-for teaching and quizzing, however, can be harmful to children, because it implies that the child does not realize what he needs to learn or how to go about learning it (Holt, 1983). Furthermore, unbidden teaching may not result in any meaningful learning because the child may not be interested in the information or skill at the moment.

Artificially contrived learning situations are often strongly resisted by young children for the reasons given above, and also because structured teaching so often fragments the world into units that are meaningless to young children. Basic academic skills are more readily and more joyfully acquired in the context of relevant, real-life activities and games.

An ideal school would have games and play equipment, books and craft activities, projects and learning centers. The children would be taken frequently to places of interest and allowed to watch people working in the real world. They would also be brought to forests, beaches, streams, mountains, and fields in order to learn about the natural world. The rest of the time they would be allowed to use and explore the materials provided, create their own fantasy play, and interact freely with each other.

The adults in this ideal school would be loving people who are able to accept children's tears and tantrums, but they would not allow the children to hurt each other or the environment. The adults would be willing to talk with the children, answer their questions, read to them, play games and work with them individually or in small groups as they explore subjects of interest.

There are many excellent nursery schools and daycare centers in the United States that come close to this description of an ideal school. There is no reason why the philosophy and environment of the nursery school cannot be extended through the early elementary grades, but many educators believe that, with students of five or six years of age, they have to begin doing something different, called "schooling." Children's natural instincts and motivation to learn are no longer trusted in most schools after the age of six. Instead, it is generally believed that children of this age must now be told what, how, where, and when to learn. This is considered to be "real learning," as opposed to the "play" that would occur spontaneously.

This attitude is harmful, because children never lose their desire to learn, and, given an appropriate environment, can continue to be self-directed learners through the elementary grades. Children do not distinguish play from learning during early childhood, because play and learning are one and the same activity for them. They learn through play, but are not aware of learning being difficult or tedious. In fact, any imposed activity that they consider to be boring will probably not result in meaningful learning at all. David Elkind claims that formal instructional programs may be as inappropriate at *all* levels of education as they are at the nursery school level (Elkind, 1973).

Based on the most recent research, The National Association for the Education of Young Children has made detailed recommendations for the type of schooling that would be most beneficial for children up to the age of eight years. For the age range from five to eight years they recommend providing an integrated curriculum with projects and learning centers that reflect children's interests, and exposing children to reading, writing, and arithmetic in relation to these activities (rather than teaching these skills as separate subjects). Art, music, movement, woodworking, dance, and drama are considered to be important parts of the curriculum. Children should be allowed to express themselves freely in these media rather than follow specific directions. They recommend allowing plenty of opportunities for play, social interaction, hands-on activities, and learning by discovery. Teachers should build on children's internal motivation to become competent and to make sense of the world without relying on the use of external rewards or punishments. Judging children's learning and work by means of letter or numerical grades is considered inappropriate. Teachers need to be aware of children's individual learning styles and rates instead of trying to mold each child into a preconceived schedule (Bredekamp, 1988).

There is a growing home-schooling movement in the United States. Many parents, uncomfortable with the educational practices and basic philosophy of schools, have chosen not to send their children to school, but are instead providing them with enriching experiences at home (including opportunities to interact with peers). There is considerable evidence by now that a stimulating home environment, responsive to children's needs, can produce highly skilled and competent children (See the journal *Growing Without Schooling* published by Holt Associates, 2269 Massachussetts Avenue, Cambridge, MA 02140, and John Holt's book, *Teach Your Own*, 1981).

What Is the Effect of Television on Young Children?

Television is an integral part of our culture, and it is here to stay. Many parents are concerned about the possible effects that television might have on their children. There is considerable evidence that television is neither a good form of entertainment nor a good source of information for young children.

Many programs for children on commercial television contain violence. Because of this, many American children have watched thousands of instances of beatings, stabbings, kickings, and shootings in their own living rooms before they enter kinder-garten. Even the "innocent" cartoons are full of characters who beat each other up and knock each other down.

In a study of eight-year-olds, it was found that the boys who watched the most violence on television were the ones who were rated the most aggressive by their peers in school (Eron, 1963; Lefkowitz et al., 1977). This correlation did not hold true for the girls, however, perhaps because of the absence on most programs of female aggressive role models.

It is not clear from these studies whether television viewing actually causes the aggressive behavior. In order to determine whether this is so, experimental studies have been made in which one group of nursery school children was shown a film displaying an adult acting in a violent manner, while another group (a control group) was shown a film without violence. Following this, the children who watched the violent film were found to act more aggressively than the children in the control group (Lovaas, 1961; Bandura et al., 1963). It can be concluded from these studies that observed violence on television does indeed increase the expression of aggression in children (Goranson, 1970).

Television viewing can also result in a desensitization to violence. Children who have been exposed to violence on televi-sion have been found to have less emotional arousal to violence (Cline et al., 1973). In other words, violence fails to upset them because they are so used to seeing it. The world would be much better off if children could be brought up to have a sense of outrage and revulsion at the sight of violence. Perhaps they would then be able to make changes for the better, instead of retreating into passivity and acceptance.

In addition to violence, television is full of frightening and suspenseful situations. These scenes openly and vividly portray children's deepest fears. Television can also be a source of new fears and misconceptions (Joseph, 1974; Osborn & Endsley, 1971). Children become addicted to frightening programs, pulled to watch them again and again in the hopes that they will somehow be able to overcome their fears (see Chapter 2). But their hopes are never realized because television promotes passivity and fails to create a therapeutic environment in which children can work through their fears.

Television provides both sound (auditory stimulation) and a moving picture (visual stimulation). This does not leave much room for a child's imagination. Children watching television are passive recipients, taking in the sensory input, but adding very little to it from their own imagination. Too much television viewing can therefore rob children of opportunities to exercise their imagination and creativity. Children watching television often appear to be in a trance-like state or stupor. This degree of passivity is neither normal nor desirable for young children (Winn, 1977).

During early childhood, time is best spent engaged in active and constructive endeavors. Television cannot be an adequate substitute for concrete, real-life activities. Instead, it runs the risk of taking valuable time away from meaningful learning. This will tend to slow down a child's intellectual development. In 1982, a survey revealed that the average American child watched television from 15 to 20 hours a week. This is two to three hours a day and represents a huge chunk out of a child's waking hours (Liebert et al., 1982).

One might assume that the constant exposure to spoken language on television would help children acquire language skills, but this does not seem to be the case. Studies have found that children who watch the most television typically have the lowest level of language skills (Burton et al, 1979; Selnow & Bettinghaus, 1982). It seems as if children do not develop linguistic skills unless they have opportunities for active communication with other people.

In addition to these drawbacks, many television programs promote a sexist attitude. The major characters are usually males, who have the most exciting adventures, the most responsibility, and the most power. There are few powerful, female role models (although the situation is gradually improving). Television contributes to the oppression and stereotyping of women by its portrayal of women as weak, dependent, stupid, passive, domestic, emotional, or as sex-objects.

Most adults consider advertisements to be a mild annoyance, but for children, advertisements have more of an impact. Ads are alluring and deceptive and cause children to crave and demand the toys or food they see portrayed. This can be a source of considerable strife and conflict in the family. Research has shown that young children do not understand the selling intent of TV commercials. They fail to realize that they are being manipulated for somebody's profit, or that the people in the ads are being paid to act. They easily assume that the ad is reality, or even a part of the program they are watching (Liebert et al., 1982). When toys are available in the stores that represent the characters seen in children's programs, then the entire program becomes a full-length advertisement for the toys. This constant exposure can make the toys seem irresistable to children.

During early childhood, children are busy trying to make sense of reality, but they also have vivid imaginations. One of their tasks, which is not easy, is to make a distinction between reality and fantasy. Television causes confusion in this area. It is not always clear to children, especially when there are real live characters, whether the story is true or invented. This confusion is further intensified by the fact that many children are exposed to the daily news on television when their parents are watching it. The news is obviously real, so why isn't everything else? It has been observed that nursery school children are convinced that the characters they watch on television really exist, even those that are animated drawings (Joseph, 1974). In an extensive study of the effects of television on children, the researchers noted this confusion between reality and fantasy and concluded that, "to young children, TV is terribly real" (Schram et al., 1961).

What Can I Do to Minimize the Effects of Television on My Child?

As consumers and concerned parents, you have the right to let the producers of children's programs know how you feel about the material presented in the programs and advertisements. If you are disturbed by the violence, racism, or sexism, do not hesitate to write letters voicing your complaints. Television is not likely to improve unless viewers take action.

It is important to keep in mind, however, that the content of the programs is only a small part of the problem. The very act of watching television is detrimental, especially to young children. When a child is "hooked" on TV, improving the programs is like giving fine wine instead of whisky to an alcoholic (Winn, 1977)! Some families, recognizing the negative influences of television, have decided not to own a television set. This is one solution to the problem. A study was done with fifteen families who agreed to turn off their TV sets for one month. After the initial difficulties in adjusting to no television, profound positive changes were noted. The children helped more around the house and yard, they read more, played outdoors more, played together more, and went to bed earlier. In general, there was a more peaceful atmosphere in the homes and a greater feeling of closeness as a family, with mealtimes being more leisurely and enjoyable (Ryan, 1974). The book *Unplugging the Plug-in Drug* by Marie Winn (1987) gives excellent suggestions for ways of limiting television viewing.

Eliminating television altogether may be too drastic a step for many families. Many parents choose to own a set because they themselves enjoy watching it. Even if a family does not own a set, the children will eventually watch programs at their friends' homes. Television is a part of our culture, and you will need to deal with its effects on your children, whether you own a set or not.

If you find yourself frequently using television as a babysitter, a first step is to search for other ways of gaining some free time. Can you afford a private babysitter for a few hours a week? Is there a relative or friend living nearby who would love to spend some time with your children? Do you know a student or elderly person who would welcome a free dinner in exchange for an hour of childcare in your own home? Are there other parents with young children in your area who also need more free time and with whom you could exchange childcare once or twice a week?

When trying to help your children limit their TV viewing, an authoritarian approach will probably not be very effective. The consequences of switching off the television with no explanation, discussion, or attention to your children's feelings can be as bad as those of letting them watch TV. The mother of a four-year-old girl told of her experience with this:

> The other day I turned off "Sesame Street" and said, "We're going to do something else now." Then I sat at my desk and Heather came up and slugged me so hard in the back, I almost fell off the chair!

One way to help children watch less television is to provide other tempting activities for them. There are many excellent books on craft, science, and cooking activities for young children. If your children have been watching television for several months or years when you begin to help them limit their viewing, you cannot expect them to become immediately self-directed. It may take them some time to overcome the passivity that television has caused, so be prepared for complaints of boredom until they learn to rely on their own inner resources. If television has become a control pattern that helps them repress their feelings, then you may need to deal with increased tears and tantrums on their part once there is less TV in their lives.

If your children insist on watching certain programs, you can watch with them. There are several reasons this can be beneficial. It allows you to know what they are watching and see their reactions to it, and it may help break the isolation and barrier that television may have created in your relationship with your children. Watching TV with your children also gives you opportunities to comment on the programs and discuss them together. This can lead to discussions of sexism, violence, and advertising. Exchanging comments during a program serves to counteract much of the passivity that is so inherent in television viewing. Finally, watching with your children will give you opportunities to help them deal with their fears and other feelings that are triggered by what they see.

If you are watching a program with your child and she seems to be afraid, you can make funny comments and encourage laughter. If a child has been very frightened by something she has seen on TV, you can encourage her to laugh or cry about it afterwards. This happened with my daughter:

> When Sarah was five years old, she had watched very little television and seen only few movies in her life. At a friend's house, one day, she watched part of a program on television that terrified her: some people were riding in a car which fell over a cliff. When she came home, she looked sad and scared. I held her close and asked her what was the matter. She burst into tears and sobbed heavily, but did not want to tell me what was bothering her. (I did not yet know.) Finally, from her comments and my own guesses, which she corrected, I learned what had frightened her. I continued holding her, and she cried in all for 35 minutes. After this, she seemed much happier and went to sleep and slept straight through the night with no nightmares. There were no residual fears from this experience. However, she did refrain from watching television again at her friend's house for several months!

The above example may seem to be an extreme reaction to television, but actually it is the normal response of a healthy child who has not been desensitized by this medium and has not learned to repress her feelings.

As a parent trying to limit TV viewing in your home, you may find that your own feelings are quite strong at times. You will benefit greatly by expressing any feelings of anger, confusion, frustration, or discouragement that you are experiencing. Try to find another adult you can use as a sounding board. Once your own feelings are out in the open, it will be easier to resist the pull towards too permissive or too authoritarian an approach, and you will be better able to come up with creative ways of dealing with television in your home.

Exercises

Explore your childhood.

1. Were you pushed to excel academically or musically? How did it make you feel?

2. Did your parents provide you with interesting learning experiences? What did they do that was helpful? What did they do that was not helpful?

3. Describe one or two of the most enjoyable learning experiences you had as a child (in or out of school).

Express your feelings about your child.

1. How do you feel about your child's current intellectual abilities?

2. Do you have a secret goal about your child's future career? Do you feel tempted to push your child academically or musically?

3. How do you feel about the influence of violence, sexism, and television on your child?

Nurture yourself.

1. Begin a hobby or learn to play a musical instrument (if this is something you have been wanting to do and have been putting off).

2. Take a class or read a book about something that interests you.

3. Are you addicted to television and would you like to watch it less? If so, take steps to limit your viewing and find more active or constructive ways to spend your time. Get support for this from other people.

CHAPTER 4: PLAYING AND PRETENDING

This chapter discusses play, one of the most important activities of early childhood. It describes how children learn through play and the ways in which play can be therapeutic. Chapter 3 described the sources of information in young children's lives, but the learning process would be incomplete without the function of play, which serves to help children assimilate and integrate their experiences.

What and How Do Children Learn Through Play?

Play has many different functions. It is generally recognized that play is an important activity of childhood, but not everyone realizes that play is much more than just "having fun." Play is vitally important because it is the primary means of learning during early childhood.

One way that play helps children learn is by offering opportunities for acquiring and practicing physical and mental skills. Play with motion such as swinging, jumping, and running helps children develop motor coordination, dexterity, strength, and endurance, and provides them with sensory experiences of movement that are important for the development of the brain (Caplan, 1973).

Many of the academic skills that children are expected to learn can be acquired through play with concrete materials. Puzzles, shape sorters, and other manipulative toys can be beneficial in helping children learn to reason, count, read, categorize, analyze, manipulate, and construct. Mathematical and logical concepts have their origin in children's self-initiated actions of grouping, sorting, ordering, stacking, and nesting (Piaget, 1965). Structured games with rules further develop children's reasoning, counting, reading, and spatial abilities, and give them experiences with cooperation, rules, taking turns, decision-making, and logical concepts such as "if-then," and "either-or." Children enjoy exercising their logical thinking abilities and often invent their own games with rules and contingencies.

An interesting study done with three- to five-year-old children demonstrates the importance of manipulative free play. Children were presented individually with the task of fishing out a prize from a box that was out of reach. In order to do so, they had to extend two sticks by clamping them together. Beforehand, some of the children were given different types of training. One group was shown the principle of clamping two sticks together, another group was given practice in fastening clamps on single sticks, and a third group watched the experimenter carry out the task. A fourth group was not given any training at all, but was simply allowed to play with the materials before being presented with the task. The children who played freely with the materials solved the task as well as the children who watched the experimenter carry out the task, and they did *better* than any of the other groups who had received training. What was particularly striking about the children who had played with the materials was their ability to resist frustration. They did not give up, even when their first attempts failed, but persisted until they had solved the problem and reached the prize (Bruner, 1975).

There is another kind of play that is of utmost importance during early childhood: fantasy play or "make-believe." When fantasy play involves two or more children, it is usually referred to as "sociodramatic play." Young children spend a good deal of time pretending. Toddlers usually begin this kind of play by their second birthday, and sometimes earlier. You may notice one day that your child moves a block along the floor and says "meow." This is the beginning of a new stage of development that Piaget has called the stage of symbolic thought (Piaget, 1962). From about eighteen months of age children are able to imagine one object representing another object. As they grow older, children can eventually construct entire pretend scenes.

Make-believe play is the child's way of practicing this new mental ability, and is an important transitional stage towards abstract symbolic thought (Vygotsky, 1967). Research has shown that sociodramatic play enhances language development. Children who engage in this kind of play with other children tend to be better story tellers and to acquire the language skills that will be needed in later school work (Pellegrini, 1986). Children also develop social skills through this kind of play, specifically how to form agreements and deal with ideas different from their own. They learn to take other children's perspectives and needs into account (Rubin & Howe, 1986). Fantasy play also enhances creativity (Pepler, 1986).

Researchers have gone further than simply providing materials for play and observing the results. Studies have also shown that when children are actually given training in imaginative fantasy play, this results in improved functioning over a wide range of behavior and abilities, including language skills, creativity, perspective-taking abilities, social problem-solving, and altruism. Training in pretend play for a period of several months was also found to cause an increase in IQ scores (Saltz & Saltz, 1986). It is clear that fantasy play is vitally important.

Children's fantasy play serves another major purpose because it is the means by which children understand and assimilate information. In the preceding chapter, I discussed how information is acquired, and how it can affect young children. But receiving input to the senses is only one half of the learning process. When we eat, we first chew and swallow, but our bodies must then spend considerable time digesting the food and eliminating waste products. It is the same with intellectual stimulation. First we take it in, then we must digest and assimilate the information so that it becomes sorted, understood, and stored in a meaningful form for later use.

Adults "digest" new information primarily by talking or writing about it. It is well known that a good way to learn and remember something is to explain it to someone else. By doing so, people can sort and organize the information, as well as relate it to what they already know. Although children do benefit by talking about their experiences, they also "digest" information by actively reconstructing it with their bodies or through the use of concrete, symbolic materials. A child who rides in a train may later pretend to be a train, draw a picture of one, or make one out of wood or paper. A child who attends a wedding is sure to have a make-believe wedding at home, and dress up as a bride or groom. When children play store, they are actively attempting to understand the meaning of money and basic economics. A child who builds a city out of blocks is involved in learning about urban living, city planning, and architecture.

When children actively reproduce the essence of their experiences through this kind of play, they are thinking, remembering, making decisions about what is meaningful, figuring out cause and effect relationships, putting related facts together, and fitting everything into their mental models of reality. This is the essence of learning (Holt, 1983). A psychologist who studied children's play extensively concluded that, "Because playing is voluntarily controlled activity..., its effects are probably intricately related to the child's mastery and integration of his experiences" (Garvey, 1977).

Children have different preferred modalities for their fantasy play. Some tend to use their whole bodies, while others prefer to build, draw, or use toys as props. My son's favorite way of assimilating information has always been to build three-dimensional models. After a boat trip to an island at the age of five, he built a model of the boat and the island out of cardboard, and taped them to a blue background representing the ocean. My daughter's way of assimilating information is more through the use of physical movements with her entire body. After a visit to Sea World (at the age of four) where she saw whales and dolphins diving into the water, she pretended to be a whale for several days, and dived into any bed that was available!

Some play is more imitative and realistic as children attempt to reproduce adult activities. When children first begin to imitate adults their play is often crude and lacking in details. A two-year-old may pretend to write out a shopping list (just like mother) by scribbling lines on a piece of paper. This degree of imitation will be sufficient for him at that stage, and he may even insist on taking his own "shopping list" to the grocery store. A child who has observed older people play and sing at the piano from music may sit at the piano, bang the keys, sing, and turn the pages of the music book from time to time. These preliminary stages of imitative play are extremely important because the children are creating frameworks into which later learning and details will fit. There is no need to push children toward more perfect imitations because they cannot assimilate everything at once.

Although fantasy and imitative play are not seen as frequently after eight years of age, these activities do not totally disappear. The play becomes transformed so that it looks less and less like play and more and more like real life or what we call "work." The following example illustrates this:

> My son went to an open alternative school from the age of five to ten. Children of all ages were in the same classroom, and free play was allowed most of the time. Over the years, Nicky and his friends enjoyed playing restaurant. As a frequent helper at the school, I was able to observe how the activity progressed as he and his friends grew older. At first, the children set up a simple restaurant and sold pretend food made out of paper, in exchange for pretend money. They did not worry about the exact amount: one piece of food was exchanged for one piece of paper money. Later on, they began to offer a written menu with prices listed. More elaborate money was produced with bills of different denominations and the children were careful to give customers change, if necessary. Then, by the time he was ten years old, he and his friends arranged with the teacher to have a restaurant for the other children consisting of *real* food. After planning and writing a shopping list, they cooked

and served a real meal in the classroom. The menu listed the food items and the prices, and bills were written stating how much each child owed. The only play element was that play money was still used (because of a school rule banning the use of real money during school hours).

In this activity, the children learned about writing numbers, adding and subtracting, writing words, basic economics, restaurant management, nutrition, planning a meal, and cooking. It also shows that there is no distinct dividing line between children's play and adult reality. As children grow older, their fantasy play gradually merges with reality until it becomes that reality. This seems to be the natural sequence of events in so-called "primitive" cultures where the children are allowed to play at adult activities such as hunting (Pearce, 1977).

Can Play Be Therapeutic?

Play is not only the primary method of learning during early childhood, it can also be therapeutic. When a child has been hurt in some way, or has experienced loss, frustration, confusion, or fear, her fantasy play will contain the elements of the experience, as described above, but it will also incorporate means by which she can release the painful emotions through laughter, crying, raging, and talking. Furthermore, in fantasy play, children can compensate symbolically for losses, mistakes, and failures in real life. A method of therapy for children called "Play Therapy" allows children to play freely in a room full of toys, with a warm, attentive therapist. It has been shown that children benefit immensely from this kind of therapy, and often make use of their time by finding ways to act out their distressing experiences through fantasy play, and to talk, laugh, and cry (Axline, 1969; Ginott, 1961; Schaefer & O'Connor, 1983, Oaklander, 1978).

Some play therapists are very non-directive, while others select materials and suggest play activities based on what they think the child needs most at the moment. The current trend in play therapy is for the therapist to use a wide range of techniques, both directive and non-directive, at different times and with different children (Schaefer, 1985).

There is a documented study that illustrates clearly how children will spontaneously deal with traumatic events in their play. At a nursery school in Pennsylvania the children observed a fatal accident just a few feet from their play yard: a man who had been repairing a street light was thrown to the ground as the piece of machinery he was standing on broke. During the entire school year following the accident, the four- and five-year-old children were seen to engage in fantasy play that included elements of falling, injury, death, and medical intervention. One of the youngest children, just three years old at the time of the accident, was unable to deal with the stress through play. A year later, still preoccupied by the accident, he had acquired fears of bodily injury, windstorms (that would make things fall down), and broken lights. Finally, by the time he was four-and-a-half years old, his play began to involve elements of the accident, such as falling down, pretending to be dead, and letting other children pretend to take him to the hospital (Brown et al., 1971).

There is some evidence that playing alone is not as effective as playing in the presence of a warm, attentive listener. Children who have experienced severe trauma have been observed to engage in a form of compulsive and ritualistic play that contains elements of the traumatic event, but does not seem to have any therapeutic benefits. This kind of play, often done secretly, has been called "posttraumatic play." For example, a four-year-old boy, whose father had been killed by a bomb and his mother hospitalized, played frequently with marble bombs and paper houses, but nobody was ever killed in his play. He was denying the reality of what had happened. His play became compulsive and did not stop until he was able to say to a therapist, "My father has been killed" (Terr, 1983).

It has been found that parents can be very effective play therapists for their children at home. A group of psychologists has trained parents to listen empathically to their children during play therapy sessions and refrain from being overly directive or analytical (Guerney et al., 1976). If your child has experienced a traumatic event, you can encourage dramatic play about the event by providing toys or props along with your own participation and loving attention. This is especially helpful if your child seems to be unable to talk or cry about the event. By means of play you can help your child face the reality of what happened and work through the feelings. The following example with my son illustrates this:

> We were having a family outing at the beach, and I announced that I was going to walk to the bathroom, assuming that Nicky, then two-and-a-half years old, would stay with the others. They were busy talking, and neither I nor they noticed when he started following me. As I returned from the bathroom and walked back to join the others, I found my very frightened and crying little boy looking for me, with some strangers trying to help him. He had not caught up with me, and could not find his way back to the others. I held him and let him cry. However, I was unable to give him my full attention because I was angry with my family for not watching him properly. A few days later I suggested going to the same beach again, but he clearly did not want to go there. I realized that he still had some painful feelings left over from the experience. I held him on my lap and asked him if he wanted to talk about what had happened, but he did not wish to. I was hoping that he would be able to talk and maybe cry some more about the traumatic incident. Since that direct approach did not work, I decided to try play therapy. I gathered together some small, wooden dolls, a small toy house, and suggested that we pretend the rug was the beach. He immediately and eagerly joined me in this "game," and we proceeded to act out together the whole traumatic event. He wanted to play it over and over again. He then changed it to be the way he had originally intended it to be in reality: he did not get lost, but caught up with me and together we went to the bathroom. He enjoyed adding props and more variations and details, and there was considerable animated talking and laughter on his part during these scenes that we re-enacted together. He continued playing the "beach game" for several days, and a few weeks later, when I suggested going to that same beach again, he was eager to go.

In this example, the opportunity to act out the scene, modify it, talk, and laugh were all important aspects of the therapy. Adults, too, benefit from re-enacting distressing scenes, as the proponents of psycho-drama have shown (Yablonsky, 1976).

To summarize, play has three major functions. One is to allow children to exercise new skills and abilities. Another is to understand and assimilate information. A third function of play is its therapeutic value in helping children overcome traumatic experiences. All three functions can be combined in a single play episode, as the following example illustrates:

> When my daughter was four years old and my son nine years old, I was hospitalized suddenly for an emergency appendectomy. They were allowed to visit me in the hospital, but the experience was nevertheless frightening for them. For about a week after my return home, the children turned the entire house into a pretend hospital, complete with an admitting office, a surgery room, a recovery room, a regular hospital room, and a hospital kitchen. Any willing visitor or family member was eagerly admitted to the "hospital." The children took people's medical histories, performed surgeries of all kinds, prepared and served pretend meals, administered medicine and wrote prescriptions. This play was accompanied by much laughter and animated talking.

In this example, the children were exercising their writing, thinking, planning, language, and social skills. They were also assimilating information about hospitals, illness, health, and medical intervention. Furthermore, their play was therapeutic in that it helped them overcome the frightening experience of their mother's hospitalization.

Once we realize the vast importance of play and recognize all of its various functions, it becomes obvious that children are brilliant models of human beings who make good use of their time!

What Is the Meaning of Imaginary Playmates and Superhero Fantasies?

Many children create imaginary playmates: people or animals with whom they speak and interact. In one survey it was found that 65% of three- and four-year-old children had such imaginary playmates. These make-believe companions usually make their appearance when the child is two to three years old, and sometimes last for several years (Pines, 1978). Some children have extremely elaborate fantasy lives and invent entire families or populations of pretend creatures.

Imaginary playmates can be a cause of concern for parents, who may feel that their child is losing touch with reality. In adults, this kind of behavior would certainly be cause for concern, but in young children imaginary playmates seem to be a sign of health rather than of mental disorder. It was found that children who had such playmates were less aggressive, more cooperative, smiled more, showed a greater ability to concentrate, were less often bored, and had richer and more advanced language abilities than children who did not (Pines, 1978). It is impossible to tell from these facts what is cause and what is effect, but, in any case, these children were clearly well-adjusted and mentally healthy.

Some children do not use their imagination in this way, but that is no cause for concern. If a child seems to be generally happy, healthy, and active, and enjoys the companionship of other children, there is no need to worry about either the presence or absence of imaginary playmates.

Just like make-believe play with real props, invisible playmates can serve the purposes of helping children understand the world, gaining control over it, and conquering their fears:

> At four years of age, my daughter, Sarah, had two invisible babies, a boy and a girl. She fed them, put them to bed, and gave them birthday parties. Sometimes they were one or two years old, sometimes three or four, and sometimes "teen-agers." Whenever we went somewhere, one or both of her babies would come along, with Sarah holding her hand. At times, Sarah was too busy to take care of her babies, so she would ask

someone else to do so. One day she announced that her baby girl was all grown up and dead. Sarah said "She's lying on the floor and can't move, and her heart isn't beating, so she must be dead. Now I only have one baby left." The next day, she had two babies again.

In this example, Sarah was using imaginary beings in order to understand growth, dependency, life, and death. Because her babies were not real, she was free to explore even the most frightening topics while maintaining absolute control over the situation.

Superhero fantasy play is also common during early childhood. The child pretends to be a well-known, powerful hero, such as Superman, or he creates his own magical character. This allows him to explore the concept of superhuman abilities such as x-ray vision, mental telepathy, superior strength, or flying. Children have little power and are acutely aware of the superior strength and knowledge of adults. They are also aware of their own imperfections and mistakes while they attempt to learn new skills. It is not surprising that they would want to play the role of an all-powerful being who is brave, strong, good, admired by everyone, never makes mistakes, and solves every problem. By pretending in this manner children can overcome some of their own feelings of fear, powerlessness, and uncertainty (Kostelnik et al., 1986).

Sometimes the favorite characters are those with evil powers, and the child pretends to kill and destroy rather than rescue others in distress. This kind of play can be a way of conquering fears. Taking on the role of a frightening and powerful monster may be the child's way of providing himself with therapeutic laughter about the very things that frighten him the most (as described in Chapter 2).

Besides having therapeutic value, superhero play can help children explore concepts of good and evil. The characters are either all good or all bad, and this simplification helps children isolate the significant values that our culture endorses or abhores. Real people are always mixtures of good and bad traits, but often for reasons too complex for children to understand easily.

What About Play That Appears to Be Senseless and Foolish?

From an adult's point of view, much of children's play appears to be silly and have no meaning or importance. A mother I interviewed described her feelings about her four-year-old daughter's silly behavior:

> It's usually right around bedtime when she becomes humorous and silly and does all these creative things like putting her pajamas on her head or her slippers on her nose. I tend to think of that as being out of control, and I give her lots of messages that it's time to be serious and to stop playing around and get ready for bed. I hear myself saying all these things and wish I could stop. It's hard for me to be fun-loving and playful with her.

Although it may be hard for parents to tolerate such behavior, silliness and laughter are extremely important for a child's development. Children have hundreds of rules of etiquette, household rules, and language rules to learn. They need to learn to dress themselves, speak properly, brush their teeth, eat with silverware, and go to the toilet. They must learn all the prohibitions and restrictions for behavior, such as not to interrupt other people's conversations, take toys from other children, draw on walls, come inside with dirty shoes, or talk with their mouth full. The list is endless. Children cannot possibly master all of these rules at once. They must be painfully aware that their behavior does not always match their parents' and society's expectations of them. Children inevitably make mistakes, and are often corrected, reprimanded, or even teased. This is why children need to play around with making mistakes and purposely doing things wrong. While being "silly" in this manner, children can then laugh and release some of the painful feelings of inadequacy, embarrassment, anxiety, or powerlessness. They are playing with the pain of others' expectations for them to do things the right way.

Once a child has mastered something new she feels confident and safe enough to face the painful feelings of not having known how to do it previously. Although the struggle to master it is over, the painful feelings still need to be released. This is why "foolishness" is often seen after a child has accomplished something new. A child who has recently learned to put her pajamas on may need to put them on incorrectly and laugh about that. A child who has recently learned to play a lotto game may need a chance to match all the cards incorrectly and laugh about that. A child who has memorized a nursery rhyme may feel the need to recite it wrong on purpose and laugh about it. Children who can change the rules in a situation where they have total control are creating a therapeutic situation for themselves. The broken rules can be of any kind, such as etiquette, games, or language (including sound, meaning, or grammar). It has been observed that much of what preschoolers laugh at is precisely this kind of situation involving an altering of actions or words to make them incorrect (Honig, 1988). To preschoolers, nonsense is not only funny, it is therapeutic.

What Kinds of Toys Are Best?

Young children need toys that allow them to use their imagination and assimilate their experiences. The toys used by play therapists are good toys for children to have in their own homes. These typically include blocks (and other building materials), sand, water, simple dolls, a doll house, puppets, toy cars, and animals. Craft materials are also important, specifically clay, crayons, and paints (including finger paints). With these materials, children can engage in the kind of fantasy play that is important for their emotional and intellectual development (Oaklander, 1978). Dress-up clothes, housekeeping toys, and doctor's kits are also helpful in stimulating fantasy play in young children.

Some parents wonder whether to give their young children realistic-looking toys that resemble real objects, such as plastic animals, dolls with detailed facial features and doll clothes, toy garages, houses, farms, a toy stove and dishes, and realistic looking cars and trucks. Or is it better to stay with unstructured, open-ended toys, such as a set of blocks and scraps of cloth, and let the children use their imagination to create their own toys? It has been shown that for very young children (under four years of age), realistic toys actually bring about more fantasy play than less realistic ones (McLoyd, 1986). Perhaps this is because the symbolizing ability of very young children is still developing, and the presence of realistic props helps to stimulate their imagina-tion. As children become older, they can gradually dispense with realistic props and rely more on their own imagination.

The children themselves can be the guide as to what toys are best for them. A fancy, highly realistic toy may please a child for a few weeks, but then end up gathering dust on the shelf, with the only harm being the expense of the purchase. On the other hand, another such toy may prove to be a favorite for many years. Children can be trusted in their play to do what they need to do. Their need for fantasy is so strong that they are not likely to allow the presence of unnecessary props to interfere, as the following example of my daughter illustrates:

> One day at three years of age, Sarah was pretending to go on a hike and a picnic. She carefully filled an imaginary backpack with invisible provisions and food. Thinking she would enjoy using a real, child-sized backpack in her play, I offered her one that I had in the closet. Upon seeing it, she became quite angry with me, stamped her feet and said very forcefully, "I don't need a backpack. I have a *pretend* backpack." Realizing her great need to fantasize, I stuffed the real backpack in the closet. I had learned a lesson!

A stimulating environment for young children should also include manipulative materials and structured toys with which they can experiment in order to learn mathematical concepts and physical laws. This can include puzzles, containers of different sizes and shapes (for water or sand play), a set of weights, a simple scale, musical instrument (such as a xylophone or a piano), rhythm instruments, sets of objects of different lengths (such as Cuisenaire number rods), and an abacus. Young children also develop intellectual skills (specifically logic and mathematics) through free play with collections they can sort and organize, such as buttons, shells, pebbles, marbles, and poker chips (Piaget, 1965). Board games and lotto games are also good materials for young children.

Additional materials useful and delightful to young children are child-sized tools and equipment (not the plastic imitations, but the kind that really work), such as a broom, mop, rake, shovel, hammer, saw, and screwdriver. With this equipment, children can participate in real work around the home. Children naturally want to help and imitate their parents. This tendency can be encouraged as soon as it appears. For children, work is not distinguished from play.

Any item that comes from the adult world can be meaningful to young children and will often be incorporated in their play. You can give your children old checks from the bank, receipt books, catalogs, menus from restaurants, coupons, advertisements, and empty food containers. These objects are like magic windows that allow children to gain access to a small part of the mysterious and complex adult world.

Should I Let My Child Play With Guns?

Some parents find gun play offensive, and do not let their children play with guns or war-like toys, while others feel there is no harm in this. Whether a child is given toy guns or not, he is quite likely to make his own out of sticks or cardboard, or simply use his fingers as a gun. It can be quite disconcerting for peace-loving parents to see their child engage in such play. The mother of a five-year-old boy said this to me:

> I don't have guns for him, but he'll use his hand or a stick. When he's over at his friend's house, they have cap guns that they carry around constantly. I don't like guns, and I've explained to them that I don't. So now, any time that he talks about guns, he'll say, "You don't like them, do you Mom, but *I* do!" My husband says that he played with guns when he was little, and he's not a violent person. In fact he is a pacifist and a conscientious objector. He doesn't see any harm in it. I guess there's no harm

in it, but I just get upset with all the toys in stores. I think it's awful. All those violent, horrible monsters and the war toys. I hate it.

As soon as children hear about wars, murders, and weapons, they will need to understand and assimilate this information, and they will also need to find a way of dealing with their fear and confusion resulting from this new awareness of human irrationality. This is especially true for boys, because children soon discover that armies are made up primarily of men. Little boys, hearing this, or seeing this on television, come to realize that it must have something to do with them, because they correctly identify themselves as males. Little girls, on the other hand, see that wars and killing do not usually involve women, so they feel this is of less concern to them. Consequently, girls do not have as great a need as boys to engage in gun play. If there were as many female soldiers involved in wars as there are male, we would probably see as many girls playing with guns as we see boys. Many parents expect little boys to be interested in guns and encourage this interest by giving them war toys. This differential treatment of boys and girls further contributes to more gun play among boys. There is no evidence of an inherent biological tendency for greater war play among boys.

Children re-enact in their fantasy play everything they hear about or observe, as described in the previous section. It is therefore not at all surprising that children will want to play pretend killing games as soon as they learn about killing in the real world. Many play therapists provide toy guns for the children they see because there is such a great need for children to play with guns (Schaefer & O'Connor, 1983). Others prefer not to provide guns but let the children create their own if they wish. Gun play indicates that the child is attempting to understand and assimilate information about killing: What is killing? How does it work? Why would a person kill another person? How would it feel to kill or be killed? What are all the different ways a person can be killed? These are some of the questions children grapple with.

Some people think that children's war-play serves only to promote wars, because it prepares children to be violent. There is no indication that this is true. Many pacifists admit to having played with guns as children. The cause and effect between war play and real wars is actually the other way around, because wars create a need for children's war play. If there were no wars or violence in the world, we would not see children playing at killing each other. They would have no need to do so.

In addition to their attempts to understand the phenomenon of violence, children also try to deal with their fears through gun play. Rather than banning this play, parents can help their children deal with these fears through laughter. If your child points a finger at you and says, "Bang, bang, you're dead!" a helpful response is to pretend to die, as dramatically as possible, and to encourage your child to laugh. If you play your part effectively, this will cause good, hard laughter, and your child will repeat the game over and over again. You will not be teaching your child to be violent. On the contrary, you will be helping him overcome some of his fear of death and violence through the tension release mechanism of laughter.

Children's gun play can also be an attempt to deal with feelings of anger and frustration. If a child feels angry towards a new sibling, some of this anger can be dissipated by symbolically killing a doll or stuffed animal that represents the baby. Anger resulting from being overcontrolled, manipulated, or punished by adults can be expressed by symbolically killing a parent with a pretend gun. In these situations, laughter can also be an additional therapeutic tool. The more the child laughs, the quicker his anger will dissipate. Parents can be helpful by acknowledging and accepting the child's feelings, and by encouraging the child to laugh.

Even though children do benefit from this kind of play, there is no need to support the war toy industry by buying war toys. These companies make huge profits by taking advantage of children's fears and their compelling need to understand violence. Children are quite capable of creating their own props with paper, cardboard, or wood. When you give your child a commercially made, realistic-looking toy gun, this can cause further confusion for the child, who may feel that his parents thereby condone guns and killing. Accepting a child's spontaneous war-play is quite different. Children know that their own, home-made facsimiles are not the real thing, and they know that the weapons have come from their own initiative and imaginations. Furthermore, when a child creates his own weapons, he can have total control over the situation, and does not have to be restricted in his play because of the appearance of his toys. A home-made sword can be turned into a magic wand at a moment's notice. Commercial war toys are too well-defined to allow for such flexibility. A plastic gun is nothing but a gun, and can be played with in only one way. If a child has had enough shooting for the day, he cannot easily change his gun into something else.

Even though you yourself do not buy war toys for your child, he may receive them as gifts from others, or he may decide to spend his own money on such items. It is not easy to keep these items out of one's home. When this began to occur in our home, although I was uncomfortable with these toys, I decided that the most respectful approach was to let my son decide which toys he wanted to own. His war play evolved over the years:

> When Nicky was five years old, he first heard about wars, and was soon making guns, swords, and bombs out of paper and cardboard, and trying them out on various members of the family. His friends at school introduced him to the popular, small war-like figures when he was about six years old, and it wasn't long before he began collecting them himself. He received them as birthday presents from his friends and spent his own money on them. He soon had quite a collection of both "good guys" and "bad guys," representing two teams at war against each other. He and his friends would spend hours at a time playing with the figures, enacting all sorts of war scenes which became more and more complex as they grew older. Then one day, when he was eight years old, the entire living room was the location of an elaborate set-up with his figures and other equipment. An unusual scene attracted my attention:

all of his figures were sitting together in a circle, both the "good guys" and the "bad guys." I asked him what was going on, and he replied, "They've decided to join forces, so they now share one big fort and they're having a conference." Apparently, evil forces were still lurking somewhere in the universe, but at least the two opposing armies on earth had overcome their animosity! If I had forbidden my son's war play, would he ever have had occasion to work out the details of a peace conference?

How Can I Be a Helpful Participant in My Child's Play?

Parents can become involved in children's play in helpful ways. Watching, listening, and responding to the child's comments make the child feel that her activities are acknowledged and accepted. At times, children request more active involvement from their parents, such as: "Will you come and buy food at my store?" It is very beneficial if a willing adult can enter into the child's fantasy world with her and be a playmate who actively participates within the structure created by the child.

Most of the time we adults expect children to accommodate to our world and to abide by our rules. When, for a change, we enter into our children's fantasy world and become an obedient playmate who participates within the structure created by them, this gives them a chance to be in control, create their own rules, and develop a feeling of powerfulness and mastery. Even when children have other children to play with, they still request, at times, adult participation in their play.

As you play with your children, don't forget the importance of laughter. Laughing together dissolves tensions and fears, and helps solidify the bond between parent and child. Most young children are quite delighted when we adults playfully pretend to be fearful, incompetent, awkward, forgetful, or weak. This usually brings hearty laughter, as it helps them release their own feelings of powerlessness resulting from being small and ignorant. Power-reversal games can be gratifying for both parents and children. In these games, the adult lets the child "push" him down, but not without a fake struggle on the part of the adult.

When your child asks you to "be the baby," she may be needing to put herself in the more powerful role of mother. If you go along with her wishes and play the role of a helpless baby, the game will probably be fun and therapeutic for your daughter.

When interacting with young children, it is tempting to direct them. This may be acceptable to children at times, but most of the time they do not need to be directed in their play, as they are perfectly capable of thinking up activities. Too many directions by adults can rob children of initiative and can even make them become dependent on adults telling them what to do.

Corrections are usually not welcome either unless the child has specifically requested feed-back about her performance. If a child has made a sign for her restaurant that says "CLOSD," and asks if she spelled it right, it is appropriate to correct the mistake. But when no information is requested, any correction may be felt as a discouragement. The child may even be angered by the fact that the adult is not paying attention to the important issue at hand, which is playing restaurant.

What if I Become Bored Playing With My Child?

Many parents would love to spend time playing with their children, but when they actually do so become restless, bored, or frustrated. The mother of a four-year-old expressed these feelings:

> Her nursery school schedule is Mondays, Wednesdays and Fridays, and I always think that on Tuesdays and Thursdays we'll have the whole day together. Well, it ends up that I usually want to do other things like clean up my desk and order from the Sears catalog that's been there for three months, and I'm not organized enough to get these things done when she's at school. When she says, "Mommy, play with me," I sit down to play with her, but then I get frustrated. I don't have the patience to play games her way, and I begin to wonder why I didn't invite some other child over to play with her! The quality time together that we dream of just doesn't happen that much.

Why is it so difficult for us parents to give children the amount and quality of attention they seem to need from us? There are probably several reasons. Young children's play is not very stimulating for adults because we have already learned the things they are learning and practicing. Playing with a child involves a tremendous amount of relaxed attention. We parents have so many worries, preoccupations, and other necessary things to attend to besides our children that we often have no more attention or time to give. Also, few of us received good quality time from our own parents when we were little and may still be yearning for attention ourselves. This can contribute to the difficulty we feel in giving good attention to our own children.

If you find yourself unable to give as much attention to your child as you would like to, you can pursue your hobbies, interests, or housework while letting your child participate in some way (as described in Chapter 3). For your own well-being as well as that of your child, it is best if you can create a balance between adult-centered activities and child-centered ones. The amount of time spent focusing on your own work and interests at home will depend on your children's ages and on their individual needs and personalities. Some children seem to need more adult participation in their play than others (especially if they do not have other children to play with).

It is also important to take care of your own needs for rest, work, exercise, time alone and with other adults. Most parents feel the need for time away from their children. There is no reason to feel guilty if you have to (or prefer to) work at an outside job, rather than spend every day with your child. Many people find that they are actually better parents with more attention for their children when they are not constantly with them. If your child is in a good school or daycare arrangement, he will be better off than spending every day with a parent who is bored, frustrated, or resentful. In an interesting survey taken of mothers it was found that mothers who would have liked an outside job, but who stayed home with their children out of a sense of duty, reported the most problems in child rearing. Fewer problems were reported by mothers who enjoyed staying home as well as by those who enjoyed going to work (Seliger, 1986). Once you have achieved a balance in your own life and taken care of your own needs, you will have better attention for your child during the times that you are together. Also, expressing your boredom and frustration (with another adult, away from your child) may help to dissipate some of these feelings and allow you to have better attention for your child. One mother reported to me how pleasurable it was when she decided to focus her attention on her three-year-old daughter (even though this was sometimes difficult for her to do):

> I've noticed that when I really decide that I'm going to give her attention, it's always a delightful experience. She'll paint and sing at the same time about all the colors she's using. It's just amazing. I love watching her. When I let her play the way she wants to, it helps me to reclaim my own past childhood memories and creativity.

How Can I Minimize the Importance of Winning and Losing Games?

Children do not normally develop a concept of winning and losing until it is taught to them. Cooperative games (in which nobody wins or loses) are initially just as much fun to young children as competitive ones. Winning becomes important only if somebody else, perhaps a parent, sibling, or friend, makes an issue of it. Children will benefit more from games if others do not take the outcome too seriously.

There is great value placed on competition in most industrial societies, and children acquire the tendency to compare their abilities and behavior with others' at an early age. They learn that they can be a winner only if someone else is a loser (Kohn, 1986).

This philosophy affects the daily lives of our children. Most sports and games are based on competition. It is difficult to find a game for children that is truly cooperative, one in which nobody wins or loses. In fact, most of us have been so thoroughly conditioned to think of all games as contests, that we cannot imagine having fun without trying to beat someone else. Our entire educational system is also permeated by competitiveness, to such an extent that it is difficult for many people to conceive of a learning or teaching situation in which nobody is trying to do better than anyone else. Yet it has been shown conclusively that people learn and perform much better in settings that are cooperative rather than competitive (Kohn, 1986).

Cross-cultural studies have shown that children differ in their tendency to be competitive, depending on which culture they live in. Seven- to nine-year-old Mexican children were found to be more cooperative in a game situation than American children of the same age. (The game was structured so that marbles could be obtained only by those using a cooperative strategy). This indicates that competitiveness is not inherent in human nature, but is acquired from growing up in a competitive culture. In an attempt to discover at what age children become competitive, the study also compared different age groups within the same American culture (children living in Los Angeles, California). Four- and five-year-old children were found to be much more cooperative in the marble game than the older ones. In fact, many of the older ones failed to obtain any marbles at all because of their strong tendency to play the game competitively (Madsen, 1971). It seems that the younger children had not yet acquired the cultural competitiveness of their environment.

Although very young children have difficulty with the concept of cooperating and taking turns, this is normally learned and mastered during the preschool years. Then, instead of a continual increase in cooperative behavior, the tendency to cooperate can become displaced by the strong influence of competitive values in certain cultures. The ability to cooperate is present in seven-year-olds, but children this age do not always choose to do so in competitive cultures such as the United States, especially when playing a game with their peers.

Cooperation can be fostered by playing non-competitive games with children. An excellent collection can be found in Terry Orlick's *Cooperative Sports and Games Books* (1978, 1982).

I have used these games with great success at my children's birthday parties, family get-togethers, and my children's school. Cooperative board games can be ordered from Animal Town Game Company (P.O. Box 2002, Santa Barbara, CA 93120). Games in which nobody wins at the expense of anyone else are extremely helpful in changing our way of thinking. It *is* possible to have fun even though nobody wins or loses. Once you have become familiar with ways of playing cooperatively, you will find that many traditional games can be slightly modified and played in a cooperative manner.

Another way to minimize the concept of winning and losing is to discourage contests in the home. When we say, "Let's see who can get ready for bed first," this makes the children compete against each other. One will win and everyone else will lose. A less competitive approach might be to say, "Let's set the timer for ten minutes and see if we can all be ready for bed before it rings."

What About Children Who Cheat at Games?

Once the concept of winning has been acquired, it invariably becomes attached to the child's sense of self-worth. Children with high self-esteem, who are secure in feeling loved, and who feel confident with their abilities, do not mind losing a game. They may even congratulate their opponent and comment about how well he played. Such children enjoy the challenges of the game and the fun of playing. The outcome is not important to them.

Children who are not as secure are often "bad losers." They may even feel so anxious about the possibility of losing a game that they cheat. It is so important to them to win the game that they risk losing popularity by infringing on the rules in order to win.

Cheating is a way that children communicate their need for assistance with feelings of incompetence. If a child is playing a game with you and begins to cheat, this is an opportunity for you to help the child with the anxious and insecure feelings he is experiencing. At such times, you can profitably turn the game into a therapy session, and forget about trying to play "seriously." Children who cheat are not ready to think about improving their strategies or to learn. They are primarily interested in the game as a means for them to release some of their pent-up feelings, so that they will be able to feel better about themselves. Children do not want to carry around feelings of anxiety about losing, and they intuitively know that the very situation that threatens them also has the resources to heal them. They will persist in trying to obtain assistance with their problem until someone has enough attention and understanding to help them. As mentioned in Chapter 2, laughter is an important tension-release mechanism for feelings of anxiety. The following example illustrates how a cheating situation can be turned into therapeutic laughter:

> I was playing a game of checkers with a six-year-old boy, but every time I was about to capture some of his checkers, he claimed that the rules did not allow me to do that. He also created queens for himself when he thought I wasn't looking. When he kept changing the rules of the game, I did not argue with him, but abided by what he said, and exaggerated the difficulties I was experiencing, saying "This is a difficult game. I don't think I'm going to win." He began to giggle. Whenever a new queen appeared on the board, I feigned surprise and said playfully, "What! Where did that come from? How did you do that?" He laughed heartily, and began cheating more and more openly. I kept him laughing throughout the entire game, and let him win.

Even children who are confident and secure enjoy changing game rules sometimes, as described in a previous section. If adults go along with them and playfully encourage laughter, the children will be able to release tensions and anxieties resulting from constant pressures on them to do things correctly. Most children have some feelings of powerlessness (resulting from infancy when they were helpless and dependent) and running a game according to their own rules gives them a chance to feel powerful in the same way that playing their own fantasy game does. Children are especially delighted when adults pretend to be helpless, ignorant, or frustrated because this creates a safe situation for them to express their own feelings of powerlessness.

Not all rule changes can be considered cheating or even a need to release painful feelings. Children are very creative and like to make up their own variations of games. Inventing games is an important form of creativity that involves a good deal of logical thought and planning. If you go along with your child's inventions, you may find yourself playing more enjoyable games than any you could buy in a store.

Exercises

Explore your childhood.

1. Did you have enough time and space to play as a child? Did you have enough (or too many) toys?

2. Do you remember your parents playing with you? Did they play with you as much as you would have liked?

3. Recall one or two of the most enjoyable play experiences you had as a child.

Express your feelings about your child.

1. How do you feel about the way your child plays? Do you ever become irritated with your child because of the way s/he plays? Do you wish your child would play with different toys or be less noisy, messy, or silly?

2. Spend one hour with your child doing exactly what your child wants to do. Talk to another adult about your feelings afterwards. Was it enjoyable? Did you become frustrated or bored? Were you tempted to teach or direct your child's activities?

Nurture yourself.

1. Buy yourself a toy or game. (This may be something you always wanted as a child but were denied.)

2. Attend a costume party, or treat yourself to an amusement park, fair, or carnival.

3. Spend time pursuing a hobby or interest of your own.

CHAPTER 5: CONFLICTS AND CHALLENGES

Children often act in ways that are a source of inconvenience, difficulty, aggravation, or concern for parents, or in ways that are dangerous or unhealthful to themselves or others. These problems are usually described as behavior requiring "discipline." This chapter focuses on the underlying causes of unacceptable behavior and offers solutions to conflicts that use neither rewards nor punishments. Sibling rivalry and problems with other children are discussed in Chapter 6.

Are Children Inherently Bad?

The notion that human beings are born with an evil nature pervades Western civilization's attitude towards children. The idea is that children are born with unacceptable impulses and tendencies that would not disappear unless the children were taught to control themselves, thereby denying their own inner nature. The proponents of this theory consider it the parents' job to civilize and tame the barbarian nature of children.

This theory assumes that children would naturally hit and bite other people, would never want to use a toilet, learn to share, cooperate, or help another person, and would lie, steal, and destroy property unless they were disciplined and taught moral values and society's rules. Parents are urged to punish children who "misbehave" so that the children will feel bad and guilty. Guilt is considered to be the great motivating force behind socially acceptable behavior. The children then learn to give up their nasty, uncivilized ways because they love their parents, want to please them, and want to be loved by them.

This belief has done more harm than any other belief invented by humanity. It is one of the main reasons the world is in such a mess. It has provided justification for violence, coercion, withdrawal of love, isolation, threats, and humiliation under the guise of "discipline." It has caused entire populations to be blindly obedient to authority figures and unable to think clearly about how to act. It has produced generations of adults who are burdened with feelings of guilt, fear, and shame. It has caused children's real needs to go unmet, producing adults who go through life trying desperately and unsuccessfully to fill their early needs, looking for someone who can love, accept, and understand them.

If we could rid ourselves of this deeply entrenched notion, if we could treat a baby from the start with an open, accepting attitude, we would be able to catch a glimpse of the real human being with a vast potential for goodness. We would see an innate tendency for physical, mental, and emotional growth, a striving to understand the world, an astounding ability to give and receive love, cooperate with other human beings, learn new skills, and acquire knowledge. We would see the capacity to reach all the higher levels of human potential.

If we were able to fill all of this baby's needs for love, understanding, stimulation, closeness, and nourishment, and if we treated her with the utmost respect and trust, we would see her grow, not into a destructive, selfish monster, but rather into a thoughtful, intelligent, cooperative, and loving adult.

When adults have tendendies towards destructiveness or violence we must assume that they were mistreated as children. People do not act in bad, stupid, or hurtful ways unless they have experienced hurtful behavior from others, or unless their needs as children were not met. Studies of criminals have repeatedly revealed severe and early mistreatments of these individuals in an environment that lacked understanding of their feelings and needs (Miller, 1983; Magid & McKelvey, 1987).

What Are the Effects of Punishment on Young Children?

A punishment is defined here as something hurtful or disagreeable done to a child in an effort to change his behavior. There are two categories of punishment: 1) doing something that is physically painful, such as spanking, beating, or whipping, and 2) depriving a child of attention, freedom, or privileges, such as isolation, or the withholding of dessert or a bedtime story.

In an article called "The Case Against Spanking," several negative consequences of spanking are listed (Gilmartin, 1979): 1) It does not alter the long-term behavior of children. 2) When used in an attempt to facilitate learning, it produces the opposite effect by creating nervousness and anxiety, thereby slowing down learning. 3) It leads to a lowered self-image. 4) Spanked children learn that the way to react to force and violence is through further and more powerful forms of force and violence. In other words, spanked children will be more likely to have violent tendencies than children who are not spanked. Boys receive three times as much corporal punishment as girls, and this could be one reason that men are more violent than women in our culture. Studies have shown that children who are frequently spanked at home are more prone to fighting and other aggressive behavior at school. 5) Corporal punishment can create social distance among family members. Children who are spanked tend to feel more alienated and less well understood by their parents and communicate with their parents less about issues of concern to them. 6) Spanked children become overdependent on external forms of control. This can lead to a lack of self-discipline. 7) Spankings during childhood can be at the root of sadomasochistic sexual feelings later on in life. 8) Children who are spanked can become resentful and distrustful of all people in positions of authority.

In an extensive study of child-rearing practices, it was found that punishing five-year-olds for aggressive acts tended to have the opposite effect of what was desired. The children only became more aggressive. The authors concluded that, "Punishment...appears to generate more hostility in the child and lead to further aggressive outbursts at some other time or place. Furthermore, when the parents punish, particularly when they employ physical punishment, they are providing a living example of the use of aggression at the very moment they are trying to teach the child not to be aggressive" (Sears, Maccoby & Levin, 1957).

If obedience is enforced very early through corporal punishment, and if the child's expressions of outrage and pain are also punished, this can have a dangerous effect. Such a child may grow into an adult who will tend to be blindly obedient to all authority figures. Early training to obey the commands of others will become second nature to him. He will lose the ability to think for himself. In her book, *For Your Own Good,* Alice Miller has analyzed the childhoods of the Nazi leaders and has concluded, "Among all the leading figures of the Third Reich, I have not been able to find a single one who did not have a strict and rigid upbringing." To the end of their lives, these people carried out every single command given to them, without hesitating or questioning (Miller, 1983).

Even when the punishment does not involve violence, as, for example, telling a child to sit in a corner, there is always the problem of having to enforce this. This involves an underlying threat of a worse consequence if the child does not obey, perhaps even an act of violence, such as a spanking. Although this may never have occurred, the child is aware of the possibility and therefore submits to the lesser punishment. Any self-respecting child brought up with a sense of his own worth will simply refuse to sit in a corner or go to his room unless he fears that something worse will happen to him if he does not. So the underlying threat of violence is often present whenever this kind of punishment is used, although this approach has been given by behaviorists the innocent-sounding label of "time-out."

Withdrawal of love or attention is also hurtful to children. Children are very vulnerable and dependent on adults for nurturing and survival. Any withdrawal of adult attention can produce considerable anxiety, confusion, and feelings of insecurity. Children need to know that their parents love them deeply and unconditionally. Even though the parent makes a distinction in his own mind between the child and his behavior, the child cannot make this same distinction. A parent may think that he is rejecting only the child's behavior, not the child himself, but the child will inevitably feel rejected and unloved. Furthermore, unacceptable behavior is often a plea for help. Children need more love and understanding at those times, not less. Deprivations of other kinds (such as not letting a child watch a favorite TV program) can lead to feelings of resentment and anger.

One study found that neither physical punishment nor withdrawal of love correlated with high levels of moral development in children. More effective in enhancing moral values were approaches that appealed to a child's feelings for other people and gave information about other people's feelings (Hoffman & Saltzstein, 1967).

All forms of punishment, whether they make overt use of violence or not, stem from an authoritarian approach in which parents use their greater power in order to create an unpleasant situation for the child. Most parents who use punishment do so with good intentions, and the pain felt by the child is thought to be inevitable in order to change his behavior and help him become a better person. No parents I have met enjoy inflicting pain on their children, but they do not know of any alternative methods that work. Non-punitive methods of dealing with unacceptable behavior are discussed elsewhere in this chapter.

There is no doubt that the use of punishment has so many negative consequences that we can no longer justify its use. It is a mistaken notion to assume that children need to be hurt or deprived in some way so that they will change their behavior, and yet this notion is so ingrained in our culture that it is difficult to rid ourselves of it. Children receive enough hurts already in their daily lives, and this is one reason unacceptable behavior occurs in the first place. To inflict additional pain in the form of punishment only adds insult to injury and will, in the long run, only result in more unacceptable behavior.

What About Rewards?

As punishment has become more and more unpopular as a disciplinary tool, many parents have found themselves resorting to the use of rewards. It is easy to assume that children can be taught to become clean, tidy, obedient, and cooperative with the use of rewards and that such an approach is more humane than one using punishment. In reality, however, the use of rewards has several hidden pitfalls.

Rewards are actually quite similar to punishments. Once a reward system exists, then the absence of a reward for misbehavior is experienced by the child as a punishment. It is a negative, unhappy experience that can result in the same negative effects as punishment, such as lowered self-esteem or anger.

Rewards can be deceptive. When we control our children's behavior with the use of rewards, we have no guarantee of instilling any values. A boy's room might be kept tidy if he is offered a piece of candy each day he cleans it up, but will he have an increased respect for orderliness, or more awareness of his environment? If fear or jealousy is causing unacceptable behavior, the use of rewards will not solve the problem in a satisfactory way and will not help the child resolve the problem.

Rewards can lead to competition. Once rewards are being offered for various deeds, competition can develop among siblings. Parents are faced with problems of deciding whether older children should receive more or fewer rewards than younger children, which tasks should be rewarded, how long to keep giving the rewards, and so on. As long as children's behavior is being measured and rewarded, any unfairness in handing out the rewards will be noticed and questioned by the children.

Rewards can backfire and have the opposite effect of what is desired. An interesting experiment demonstrated that preschool children who received an expected reward after doing a drawing activity subsequently lost interest in the activity when the reward was removed. On the other hand, children who were never rewarded in the first place did not lose interest (Lepper et al., 1973). It seems that when rewards are given, children begin to perform in order to obtain the reward and lose touch with their original interests and desire to learn. A similar result could occur with helping around the house. Rewards can also cause children to "misbehave" in a conscious effort to make their parents continue feeling the need to give rewards. As one little boy explained it, "I get what I want by keeping mother thinking I'll be bad. Of course, I have to be bad often enough to convince her she is not paying me for nothing" (Baruch, 1949).

Another disadvantage of the use of rewards is that it teaches children to follow the pleasure/pain principle. Behavior modification approaches that rely on promises of rewards or threats of punishment teach children that it is acceptable to do whatever brings about a pleasurable event or avoid doing what causes a disagreeable one. This conditioning may then come to replace the ability to think clearly about how to act and to take long-term consequences into account. If adults were to base their actions on this pleasure/pain principle, they would do whatever resulted in an immediate reward. Momentary thrills, such as those caused by drugs and new possessions, may be tempting to people subjected to this kind of childhood conditioning. Our job as parents should be to teach our children how *not* to be manipulated by anything or anyone, including advertisements, drugs, peers, authority figures, or ourselves, no matter how alluring the rewards appear to be. Our task is to help our children develop the ability to think for themselves about how to act, and to keep on thinking when others try to manipulate them with alluring rewards. The use of gold stars, candy, TV, stickers, money, or any other manipulative device, innocent as it might seem, is a clear message to our children that it is okay to let others control their behavior and their lives.

A final negative effect of the use of rewards is that it can be felt as an insult by children. Human beings have the ability to think creatively and intelligently about how to act. Even very young children can think well about how to behave when all their needs are met. When we try to modify children's behavior with the use of rewards we communicate that we do not think they are smart enough to figure out for themselves the right way to behave or to understand our logical explanations. It indicates to them that we do not trust their inherent ability to grow and learn.

There are some situations in which young children enjoy receiving rewards for doing things. In the scouting movement, merit badges are earned for accomplishing specific tasks, and children's libraries sometimes offer reading programs in which a sticker or other prize is given for each book read. As long as the children can *choose* to put themselves into this kind of contingency situation, it will be experienced very much like a game and will not have the negative consequences of rewards discussed in this section. The various pitfalls are much more likely to occur when the children have no choice and when the reward system is imposed by an authority figure in order to control a child's behavior.

The following sections of this chapter offer several suggestions for dealing with unacceptable behavior and eliciting cooperation in young children without resorting to the use of either rewards or punishments. Our role as parents is not to train our children like circus animals, but to treat them with respect and integrity so that their natural ability to think well and guide themselves will flourish.

Why Do Children Misbehave?

Children are not inherently bad, but they do sometimes act in ways that are uncooperative, annoying, hurtful, destructive, or dangerous. When children act in these ways it is an indication of something having gone wrong. There are three major reasons for unacceptable behavior.

The child is experiencing a need. Unrecognized and unfilled needs can cause children to act in ways that are unacceptable to others. As an illustration, a hungry little girl whose father is busy reading the newspaper, may, after several unsuccessful attempts to gain his attention, begin teasing her baby brother to make him cry. Physical needs such as hunger cannot be put off easily by young children.

The need for attention is another legitimate need, and children who do not get enough are going to find ways of making themselves noticed. If their behavior results in increased attention it will have served its purpose, even though it may have been unacceptable to the parents.

There are other important needs besides food and attention. Children have a great curiosity and desire to explore, touch, and manipulate. When this need is repeatedly frustrated by taking children to places where no touching or exploring is allowed, unacceptable behavior is likely to occur.

Unfortunately, most public places do not take children's needs into account, and parents are not given much help or support when waiting in restaurants, stores, post offices, or banks with young children. The children become bored and begin to provide their own stimulation with whatever is available. If the children's continuing need for stimulation is recognized it is often possible to fill that need in ways that are acceptable to adults. Suggestions for doing this are described in a later section.

The child has insufficient information. Conflicts often arise because children have insufficient information about the consequences of their behavior. When a young child walks into a house with muddy shoes, perhaps he does not have sufficient information about the way mud sticks to shoes, comes off on rugs, or about the difficulty of cleaning rugs. Perhaps he does not even know that his shoes are muddy. Before assuming that a child is "naughty," it is important to check for possible misunderstanding or lack of information.

The child is harboring painful, pent-up feelings. When a child hits or bites other people in a deliberate attempt to inflict pain on them, we are dealing with a third reason for misbehavior. Children who act in ways that are obnoxious, uncooperative, spiteful, violent, or destructive are feeling bad. They have pent-up feelings of anger, fear, or grief that result from previous distressing experiences.

Children experience hurts, frights, and frustrations on a daily basis, even in the most loving environment. If children's painful feelings are repressed, their behavior can then easily become distorted and unacceptable (See Table 1 in Chapter 1). These feelings need a harmless outlet, and the children need attention so that they can release the accumulated tensions by crying and raging. No amount of punishment, preaching, or distraction will be effective in curing the underlying cause for this kind of behavior. Only the opportunity to release feelings freely will produce positive results. Children who act out their distress in obnoxious and violent ways are actually very close to tears, and often a firm but loving interruption of the child's distorted behavior is sufficient to allow a genuine release of feelings to occur (Heron, 1977). Examples of this are given in later sections of this chapter.

Unacceptable behavior can often be considered a child's plea for help. It is sometimes the only way children can think of to ask for help with the overwhelming feelings they are experiencing at the moment. Although they may not be consciously aware of choosing to act in these ways, the purpose of their behavior is very often to make somebody notice them, understand how bad they are feeling, and take steps to make it safe enough for them to release their pent-up feelings.

Parents can expect to see their children at their worst because children "act up" with the people with whom they feel the safest. They are essentially saying to their parents: "You care about me more than anyone else, so I'm waving this red flag to show you how bad I'm feeling, in hopes that you will be able to help me release these feelings and overcome them." A child whose fears come up at night cannot be expected to say, "I'm terrified of death and I feel it the most when I'm alone in bed." Life would be much easier if children could communicate verbally in this manner. Instead, they may become uncooperative, aggressive, or overly demanding at bedtime. Such behavior is a clue for parents. It indicates that this is an area of distress for the child and that assistance with the feelings is needed.

In these situations children do not always receive the kind of attention they need, because their behavior is understandably quite upsetting and baffling to parents. It is tempting to want to stop the behavior at all costs and easy to forget that the child is feeling hurt or scared. It is important to stop unacceptable behavior, but if this is done without opportunities for the child to express his feelings, he will continue to feel bad and the behavior will tend to recur.

Can Unacceptable Behavior Be Prevented?

It is possible to take certain steps that will minimize conflicts and help prevent unacceptable behavior. Here are some guidelines to keep in mind:

1) Give plenty of closeness and individual attention. Children are much less demanding and disruptive if these vital needs are being regularly met.

2) Encourage your child to release feelings regularly by crying and raging. Much unacceptable behavior will simply not occur if painful feelings have a frequent outlet.

3) Create a child-proof and child-friendly environment. Child-proofing is extremely important during the infant and toddler stages, but some amount of child-proofing continues to be helpful and necessary during the preschool years as well. Poisonous chemicals and cleaning materials should still be kept out of reach, as well as precious or breakable objects. A television set in plain view is tempting to turn on, whereas one inside a cabinet or in a less frequented room is not as likely to be used.

Children need things to do. Much unacceptable behavior can be prevented in waiting rooms, grocery stores, and on long trips by bringing along small toys and snacks for young children. Even in their own homes, children can become bored with their toys. One way to prevent this is to keep some toys and games out of sight and give them to the children when they seem to need new stimulation. I reserved special toys for times that I received important telephone calls, and handed them to my children at those times so that I could be guaranteed not to be interrupted.

Another way of making the environment suitable for young children is to make changes that will help the children be self-sufficient. Children will be more likely to hang up their own coats if they can easily reach the hooks or to serve themselves their own cereal and milk if they can reach the bowls and spoons and pour the milk.

Finally, a child-friendly environment is one in which the child does not need to wait very long for food and drink when hungry and thirsty.

4) Prepare your child for what is expected. If you are planning a dinner party, let your child know ahead of time what to expect and what you expect from her. Rehearse new situations beforehand, such as a visit to the dentist, a first day at school, a new baby sitter, or a train trip.

5) Limit the use of commands. Orders and commands are usually strongly resisted by young children because this deprives them of freedom to make their own choices about what to do. Furthermore, the only way to enforce a command (that goes against a child's wishes) is with the use of either rewards or punishments. As described in previous sections, these techniques have many pitfalls and negative consequences. It is impossible to *make* a child do something without being oppressive in some way. Prohibitions, on the other hand, are easier to enforce and are also more readily accepted by children, because they allow children to maintain a certain amount of freedom of choice (Holt, 1984). Conflicts can often be avoided by using prohibitions instead of commands. Instead of telling a child he has to play in his room for an hour, you can tell him that *you* are going to be working in *your* room for an hour, and request that he not bother you. He is then free to play in any room except yours.

6) Give choices. Another alternative to commands is to provide children with choices: "Shall we read this story before or after

you brush your teeth?" "Would you like to wear your blue or red pants today?" Children are more likely to cooperate with parental wishes when they have a sense of choice.

What Can I Do When My Child's Behavior Is Unacceptable?

It is never possible to prevent all conflicts. Children lack important information, unforeseen circumstances occur, new needs keep appearing, we overestimate our children's abilities to understand and remember rules, and feelings such as fear, frustration, grief, and jealousy interfere with children's ability to think clearly about how to behave. A previous section described the three major reasons for misbehavior: 1) A need is being felt, 2) The child lacks information, and 3) The child is experiencing some painful feelings. The first step to take for any unacceptable behavior is to try to determine which of the three causes applies.

You can begin by asking yourself: "What does my child need right now?" Once you have determined this, you can try to suggest alternative activities to your child that allow her to fill her need in ways that are acceptable to you.

Sometimes very little is required to fill a child's need, as the following example with my daughter illustrates:

> When Sarah was three years old, she would often come to the dinner table without having washed her hands and would refuse to wash her hands when I asked her to do so. I could have withheld dinner until she did so or given her a penny each time she remembered to wash her hands. These would have been authoritarian approaches that put me in the position of controller and manipulator. Instead, I tried to put myself in her place. Often, she was very hungry and did not want to be bothered about washing hands. It was difficult for her to postpone eating once she had seen all the food. Also, it seemed very important to her to have her own way and to not submit to my authority. The solution I found was to tell her she could have one bite of food before washing her hands. This always worked, and she

would wash her hands without any further protests. Eventually, she learned to remember to wash her hands before eating.

I used to wonder why this approach worked so well. I think that its effectiveness resided in the fact that it turned a confrontation of wills into a situation in which nobody was the loser. It allowed her to "save face." Even though I gave in to her wishes in a very small, almost symbolic way, it was sufficient to make her feel that her needs were being met and her feelings understood.

Sometimes solutions are not so easy to find because the child has a legitimate need that conflicts with the parents' legitimate needs. There are two traditional approaches for dealing with this kind of conflict. In the authoritarian approach, the parent uses rewards or punishments (or promises and threats) to compel the child to act in a way that allows the parent's needs to be met. The child is the loser and the parent is the winner of the conflict. In the permissive approach, the parents give in and let the child's needs be filled at the expense of their own needs. The child is the winner and the parents are the losers. Neither of these situations is satisfactory because the children become resentful when an authoritarian approach is used, and the parents become resentful when an overly permissive approach is used.

The solution is to try to fill everybody's needs. The parents can let the child know that her needs are recognized and understood, and they can also let her know what their own needs are. The child can then be asked to help think of a solution that would satisfy everybody. Even very young children can be quite helpful in thinking of creative solutions to conflicts like these if parents give them a chance. The book *Parent Effectiveness Training* has many examples of conflicts solved in this manner (Gordon, 1975).

The following example illustrates how my first authoritarian attempt at solving a conflict-of-needs situation led to anger and aggression in my daughter:

When Sarah was six years old, she liked to get dressed on cold mornings in the bathroom with the electric heater on. However, she dawdled and wanted the heater on for a long time. This aggravated me because I resented the cost of the electricity. I would go in after about five minutes and turn the heater off. This resulted in a screaming rage on her part because she hadn't finished getting dressed. No amount of explaining about the cost of electricity seemed to help. She still dawdled. One time she was so angry at me after I turned the heater off that she hit me. From her point of view, I was being quite mean. I realized then that I was dealing with her in an authoritarian and disrespectful manner, and that there must be a better way to solve our conflict. I discussed the problem with her, but she could not think of a solution, so I suggested that I set a timer in the bathroom for five minutes and leave the heater on until the timer rang. She liked the idea of knowing exactly how much time she had, but wanted to negotiate about the length of time. Finally, we agreed on five-and-a-half minutes! This worked beautifully. She always dressed quickly from then on and never complained when the bell rang and I turned the heater off. In fact, she was often dressed *before* the bell rang and said, "You can turn the heater off now."

A common problem with young children is frequent demands for attention. Children have a legitimate need for attention, but parents also have needs. Between the ages of two and eight years, children gradually come to understand that other people have needs. These needs can be explained to children, while at the same time recognizing the children's needs for attention. When everyone's needs are recognized, then solutions can often be found that fill the needs. An agreement might involve having the children help with chores so that their parents will have more time to play a game or read to them. The children are not compelled to do these things. Instead, the solutions are reached by mutual agreement. (This approach cannot be expected to work very well with children under the age of four years.)

The second possible reason for unacceptable behavior is the fact that young children lack information. It is easy to forget how uninformed little children really are. They know nothing about our complex world until they experience it or until the facts are explained to them. I learned this from an example with my son:

One day, when Nicky was two years old, he was playing quietly, and I went to see what he was doing. To my horror, I found him busily coloring the wall with his crayons. Although I was quite upset by this, I realized that he did not have the information I had about crayons and walls. I said that I wanted the wall to stay white, and I began scrubbing it clean. I encouraged him to help me clean the wall, which he did quite willingly. It took us about an hour of hard work to clean it up. I then explained again that we color only on paper, not on walls, and I made sure that he always had a stack of paper. He never colored on the wall again.

At no point in this episode was my son made to feel bad or guilty about what he had done. I simply gave him the information that he was lacking by letting him see how much work it was to get the crayon marks off the wall. This was done cheerfully and matter-of-factly.

In this example, my son was old enough to understand the concept of a rule: what was true for that day applied to every day and every wall. Children under the age of two years cannot be expected to learn rules governing their own behavior, and each conflict must be dealt with as if it were entirely new. (Ways of doing this are discussed in my book, *The Aware Baby*.)

One way of providing a child with necessary information is to let natural consequences occur, if this is possible and appropriate. Here is an example:

When Sarah was four years old, she took daily swimming lessons for a few weeks. I became irritated by the fact that she never hung up her swimming suit and towel after we got home, but left them on the floor. I usually hung them up for her, until I realized that it was her responsibility, and that the reason she did not do it herself was probably that she had never experienced putting on a wet bathing suit. I explained to her that her bathing suit would still be wet the following day if she did not hang it up. She did not seem to care, so I left it and her towel in a heap on the floor. The following day she was upset at having a wet bathing suit and towel. After that, she hung them up herself.

It seemed that the only way for my daughter to acquire the necessary information in that situation was to let her experience the discomfort of a wet bathing suit and towel. Sometimes information is learned unpleasantly, and we parents do not always have to shield children from the consequences of their own actions if we feel that meaningful learning will result from this information. At these times, the most effective approach is to do nothing at all and let the consequences occur. When this approach is used, the parent's attitude is very important. If I had said, "I told you that would happen," this may have caused my daughter to feel like a loser and to be resentful and angry. A more helpful approach is to try to remain objective and to be truly sympathetic when the child experiences a disagreeable consequence of her own making. Any crying or raging needs to be accepted, and the child's feelings lovingly acknowledged.

There will be occasions when natural consequences are too dangerous. In these situations, other ways must be found to convey the necessary information. If a young child continues to run into the street after you have explained the dangers, then perhaps showing a picture of a child hit by a car or pointing out an animal on the road that has been hit by a car will help convey the necessary information. If your child still does not understand, it will be necessary to provide supervision or restraints (such as a fence or staying indoors unless an adult is with the child). When punishment is used, children may learn to obey and follow the rules, but you will probably not want to rely solely on their obedience in situations as dangerous as a busy street. Since you will need to supervise anyway, it is best to avoid punishing altogether, and wait until the child is old enough to understand the dangers involved before trusting her to stay on the sidewalk.

How Can I Deal with Unacceptable Behavior Caused by Pent-up Feelings?

If a child continues to act unacceptably after you have tried to take all possible needs into consideration, and after you have given all the necessary information you can think of, it is quite possible that your child is harboring painful feelings that are causing him to act unacceptably. Destructive, obnoxious, and other unacceptable behavior often occurs when children have pent-up fears and frustrations.

A common response to this kind of behavior is to withdraw love and attention. It is believed that the child who is ignored will learn that he cannot gain the attention he is seeking by acting that way. However, children desperately need attention at such times, and ignoring the child will not make the problem disappear. Not just any form of attention will work, however. The kind of attention required must address the issue in such a way that the child will no longer feel pulled to act unacceptably.

There are two guidelines to follow in this kind of situation. The first is to stop the unacceptable behavior in a way that does not hurt or humiliate the child. Yelling and spanking will not be effective in the long run and will only give the child more painful feelings to deal with. A firm statement of limits is sufficient at times, for example, "You may not kick the window." At other times, you may need to use your greater strength (but not violence), for example, firmly restraining a child who is hitting another child, or removing from a child's hand an object that is being used destructively.

The next step is to allow and encourage a release of feelings. When a child is acting unacceptably because of painful feelings, stopping the behavior often brings about a spontaneous release through crying and raging. This crying is the actual cure that will prevent the behavior from recurring.

Children need to bounce their feelings off of someone who can patiently listen to their outpouring of emotions without becoming either angry or frightened. Sometimes they need someone big and strong to push and struggle against, who can hold them firmly and absorb their rage. After the child's storm has passed, parents will find themselves holding a much relieved and relaxed little person who will be loving and cooperative with no trace of tendencies towards destructive behavior. This approach has been used very successfully with severely disturbed children who act out their anger in violent ways. These children have suffered from abuse or neglect during infancy. The therapist firmly holds the child in order to encourage a rage reaction with crying and screaming. Profound changes are noticed, sometimes within a matter of hours (Magid & McKelvey, 1987).

Even though children may not have been abused or neglected, they still accumulate many painful feelings that cause them to act in violent, obnoxious, and uncooperative ways. Loving but firm holding can be very effective and beneficial both in stopping the unacceptable behavior and in helping the child release pent-up feelings. The following example illustrates the use of firm holding with my son:

> One day at four years of age Nicky was acting very obnoxiously. He kept slapping the newspaper that his father was trying to read and then came over to me and started slapping me. It seemed clear to me that he was asking for assistance with some painful feelings, so I brought him into the bedroom and held him tightly. He struggled and then soon started to cry. I held him and caressed his face lovingly while he screamed and cried hard. He kept asking for things, for example, he wanted dinner, and he said he had to go to the bathroom. I told him gently that all those things could wait, and that I was going to hold him for a while. He cried hard for about 15 minutes and then calmed down and almost fell asleep. Then he told me a nightmare he had had the previous night about thieves coming into the house. After that, he wanted to cuddle with me some more. He was delightful the rest of the day with no trace of obnoxious behavior.

The use of firm holding is quite different from the use of punishment because there is no attempt to hurt, humiliate, threaten, or deprive the child, and there is no withdrawal of love. The attitude towards the child is one of respect, while at the same time recognizing that the child's behavior is unacceptable. The child is spoken to gently at all times, and the child's feelings are acknowledged and accepted. The parent conveys the attitude that the child is a good, lovable person. The use of firm holding creates a safe place for children to vent their feelings harmlessly and should never be done in the spirit of anger or punishment.

There are other ways of helping children release their feelings when they are acting destructively or unacceptably. One way is to act playful and encourage laughter. This can be especially useful if a child seems to be unable to cry. The laughter may then be followed by spontaneous crying. A woman wrote to me of her experience using a playful approach with a two-year-old boy she took care of regularly, who was acting quite obnoxiously with her:

At Christmas we were away from one another for a week, and when we were back together, Jason seemed very much not at peace with himself, yet had stopped crying altogether. If I held him, he wouldn't cry. He was whiny and fussy and often angrily said that he wanted things. The things he requested did not seem to satisfy him, and he sometimes tried to hit me. I sensed that he had a lot of pent-up distress, but he seemed too afraid to "let go" with me. His father had temporarily moved out, and Jason was probably feeling terrified. I decided to use a more playful approach and to encourage laughter. One day, we had been at a skating rink and it was time to go but Jason did not want to go. In the car, he said very "brattily" and angrily, "I want to stay at the skating rink." I acted silly and mimicked him while making a very goofy face and showing as much acceptance as possible. I was trying to convey that his anger did not upset or unravel me, that there was plenty of room for it, and I wouldn't take it personally. In seconds of our continuing on in this way, he was laughing his head off, and seemed more relaxed with me than he had been in weeks. The whining decreased and he seemed much less angry. Each time he was angry, I would be light and playful and silly with him.

The next day, we were outside in the snow and he started to get very frustrated going up a hill and began whining. I continued being silly and light, and then Jason began wailing spontaneously and so much came out! I just got down at his level and gave him my attention. His sobbing sounded more like grieving than anger. I nearly cried with joy myself, because it seemed to free him so. It was the first time in over six weeks that he had cried. I was certain that he really had needed to, but that he just couldn't feel safe enough to do so. The difference in disposition immediately after that was phenomenal. He became calm, natural, peaceful, and happy. All clinging and demandingness ceased. It was really something.

When a playful approach is used, great care must be taken so that the child understands he is not being teased.

Many parents resort to punishment when their child is acting in the ways described above. A spanking does sometimes succeed in stopping unacceptable behavior and allowing the child to begin crying, but it accomplishes this at a great cost to the child's self-esteem and to the parent/child relationship.

Sometimes unacceptable behavior occurs because children actively resist adult authority or overcontrol. Children can be expected to obey reasonable and occasional prohibitions based on the parents' greater knowledge and experience. But a child treated in an authoritarian manner, or who is overly restricted in situations that are not really dangerous, may come to stop heeding parental warnings even in situations that *are* dangerous (such as going too near the unsteady edge of a cliff). Rebellious and self-endangering activities occur in these situations because the child is not thinking clearly. He is too preoccupied with his frustrations and his desperate need to assert his independence. These children need to have their unacceptable behavior stopped and they may need assistance in releasing pent-up feelings (as described in this section). However, this may lead to only temporary improvement because the parents need to change and become generally more accepting of their children.

If your child frequently resists your warnings and prohibitions in situations that are potentially harmful to himself or others, it may be wise to check if you are being generally too restrictive of him (at other times). If you think that this is the case, then any counseling or therapy you can obtain may help to improve the situation. You may need to work through your fears about your child's safety, or your need to control your child (just as you yourself were controlled when young). This will ultimately help you become more relaxed and less restrictive with your child and will lessen his tendency to assert himself in dangerous or clearly inappropriate ways.

I Sometimes Hurt My Child and Then Regret It. What Can I Do About This?

There are several reasons why parents lose their tempers and act punitively and hurtfully towards their children. The major reason is that most of us were punished ourselves when we were children and were made to feel that it was "for our own good."

The second reason is that, after being punished, our expressions of outrage and pain were repressed. This has resulted in a double hurt: the original punishment and the inability to express the hurt feelings resulting from the punishment. We had no choice but to repress our painful feelings. The consequence is that we then tend to justify the use of punishment and treat our own children in exactly the same way (Miller, 1984). Even when we feel that our own punishment was unjustified, if our feelings of pain, resentment, fear, and anger have not been fully released, there will be a strong pull for us to act in similar hurtful ways when our children irritate us.

This kind of childhood experience leads to the widespread belief that, unless children are used to frustrations, deprivation, and mistreatments when they are little, they will not be well prepared for the real world. It is felt that it is better for children to be hurt by someone who loves them than to grow up and be knocked down by someone who does not.

Although well-intentioned and stemming from parents' deep love and concern, this reasoning is not correct, because it is based on the assumption that the best preparation for a bad experience is a bad experience. If a famine were predicted for the future, parents, using this logic, would deprive a child of food before the famine had even begun. This is obviously illogical. The correct approach would be to give children the best nutrition available so that their bodies would grow up to be healthy and strong and thereby stand a better chance of surviving a famine.

The same can be said for psychological needs. If you are concerned about your children's future in a tough world, the best preparation you can give them is psychological health, which can only occur when they are treated with love, trust, and respect.

Children who feel self-confident, proud, and powerful stand a far better chance of surviving, thriving, and even of changing our oppressive society, than those who have been hurt and humiliated through the use of punishment.

This may be especially difficult for certain groups of people to accept. Any religious, racial, or ethnic group with a history of slavery or oppression may have a deep-rooted fear, passed on to them by their own parents, that their children will not survive if they are brought up to be proud, confident, and bold enough to question authority. In the past, punitive methods of child-rearing may have been necessary because the children's very survival depended on their willingness to be obedient and submissive. The terror and the authoritarian patterns of child-rearing can be passed on from generation to generation even when present conditions may be less oppressive than they used to be.

Another reason for our hurtful behavior is the fact that we parents are simply emotionally and physically exhausted much of the time. There are many causes of stress for parents, including financial problems, housing, and marital conflicts. Additionally, we do not usually have much support or help with the job of day-to-day parenting. In an ideal society, no parent would be required to care for a child when she herself is ill, tired, or emotionally drained. There would be ample resources to call on in times of need. Parents are expected to be perfect, and this is a cause of guilt and anxiety. When children develop emotional or behavioral problems, parents are the first to be blamed. Yet our society does not offer parents the training or support they would need to do a better job.

In spite of these various difficulties, I firmly believe that it is possible to treat one's own children better than oneself was treated. Every parent is struggling to do this because nobody wants to inflict pain on their own children. I am continually amazed at the inner resources and strength of the parents I have worked with, who are doing everything possible to give their children the very best upbringing they can offer, in spite of their own past history of being punished, abused, or neglected, and in spite of great financial difficulties.

There are some steps you can take if you find yourself frequently hurting your child. One is to find an outlet for your own feelings by joining a support group, obtaining counseling or therapy, finding a friend you can talk to about your feelings, or calling a child abuse hot-line. It will be most helpful if you can begin to remember how you yourself felt as a child and to express openly any resentment or anger about the way you were treated.

The second step you can take is to ask for help with the actual job of parenting. You do not have to do the job alone. If money is short, there is always the possibility of exchanging child-care with other families, so that you will have some time away from your children.

When all else fails, and you find yourself about to do something hurtful to your child, you can leave the room, hit a pillow, yell into a pillow, cry, or call a friend and talk about how you are feeling. Some people hold their breath and count to ten. This might help temporarily, but it is much healthier for you if you can let your feelings out rather than hold them in.

Children do bring up strong feelings in their parents and can be extremely irritating. If parents can harmlessly release the feelings of anger that are triggered by their children's behavior, they will be able to think more clearly and deal with unacceptable behavior in creative and effective ways that do not cause the children harm.

If you have struck your child in anger and feel guilty and remorseful, hug your child, tell her you love her, and explain to her that sometimes you do things that you do not really want to do, because you cannot always control yourself. You can explain that she did not deserve to be hit, and that she is a good person. Also, give her a chance to tell you how she felt and to cry and rage about it if she needs to. Do not be surprised if she says she hates you or claims that you are mean. This is a healthy and necessary reaction. Your own feelings, too, will need an outlet. Instead of keeping your guilt to yourself, you can allow yourself to cry. This will be much healthier for you than keeping your guilt feelings bottled up inside. It is best if you can find another adult who is willing to hear you out and who will not condemn you for having hit your child. A mother reported to me an experience of hitting her four-year-old daughter:

> One time I remember, I had just bought her some cards, and we were playing cards, and she started crunching up her cards. I was so shocked that I hit her hand. Well, she went into hysterics and cried very hard. Afterwards we had a talk, and I explained to her, as the tears were coming down my face, that I should have used my words. She seemed to really understand that I had something to work on. I didn't know how to use my words, and using words is a lot better than hitting.

Remember to pat yourself privately on the back for all the times you did *not* hit your child, even though you felt a strong urge to do so. You need to be applauded for those times of self-control.

How Can I Get My Child to Help With Household Chores?

Young children normally imitate everything they see their parents do, including chores around the house. If you encourage this tendency at an early age by giving your toddler a small broom, mop, rake, shovel, and other tools similar to those that you yourself use around your home or yard, then your child will be more likely to want to be helpful later on. At first, a two-year-old's attempts to mop the floor will not be very helpful, and chores may take a little longer when you do them together with your young children. But your patience will pay off in the long run. Toddlers who are told they are in the way or sternly reprimanded for mopping the windows instead of the floor, will soon give up trying to do chores with you.

As children become older, cooperation is more likely to occur if you continue to do chores together. "Let's see how quickly we can rake this yard together." Also, stating a joint goal can make chores seem more meaningful and fun: "Let's surprise Daddy by washing all the windows today." Giving specific choices is also helpful because it lets children know exactly what needs to be done, and because they can be active in selecting what they do. This will make them more likely to cooperate: "Let's clean up your room today. Would you like to start by finding all the blocks or all the doll clothes?" Chores can be made fun by talking, singing, or making a game out of them. You can set a timer and try to beat the clock, or put on a record and attempt to finish a specific task before the music stops.

Let children know that their help is invaluable. When my daughter was four years old, her little mop fit behind the toilet, but my big mop did not. I told her this, and she was always eager to mop the bathroom floor while I mopped the kitchen floor. It is also important to appreciate children for helping and let them know that their help allows you more time and energy to do other things with them.

Children do not begin life with a concept of a distinction between work and play. Everything is fun for them at first, including those tasks we have come to think of as jobs or chores. We adults often have negative attitudes towards household chores, perhaps because of having been forced to do them as children in an atmosphere that lacked cooperation and fun. Also, women have traditionally been oppressed by having to do all the household chores with no recognition or financial recompense. Chores have come to mean disagreeable work to many adults. If you yourself hate housework, it will be understandably difficult to convey a relaxed, fun attitude about it to your own children, and you may find yourself nagging them to help and threatening them if they do not. Your children, in turn, may acquire a similar distaste for housework. This vicious cycle may be difficult to break until you work through your own feelings about housework. I experienced difficulty with a specific chore because of my childhood experiences:

> The part of housework that I dislike the most is making beds. When I was little I had to help make the beds, and my mother was very particular about how it was to be done, and also very critical. It was not at all fun. Not surprisingly, I had very little

patience with my children's first clumsy attempts to help me. My own irritation with them caused them to begin "acting up " when I tried to make the beds. They would jump on the bed, hide under the sheet, and so on. The only way I could do this chore without entering into conflicts with my children was to send them out of the room, or do it at a time when they were not at home. It was obvious to me that I had some painful feelings from my own childhood that needed to be expressed. After I did this (with the help of a peer counselor), I was able to be more relaxed about making beds.

To conclude, the only way children will help with household chores is if we can win them over to "our side" (Ginott, 1965).When children are respected and treated as equals in the home, when they are not expected to comply with the power and authority of adults, and when a joyful attitude towards cleaning and organizing is communicated, there will emerge the kind of cooperation that is based on love and trust, and the mutual desire to keep the home clean, orderly, and beautiful. Children will spontaneously assume the kinds of responsibilities we want them to have.

What Can I Do About Bedtime and Naptime Problems?

Bedtime problems rank high on the list of difficulties with young children. Much resistance to bedtime can be avoided by paying attention to children's needs. Most children of preschool age still need to fall asleep in the presence of another person and resist being alone. This is an innate tendency that we human beings share with all mammals. Young mammals do not fall asleep away from their mothers but stay near them for warmth and protection. There is nothing wrong with catering to this need if your child requests your company at bedtime until he is asleep. As mentioned in Chapter 2, fears are common at this age, and are especially likely to surface when the child is alone in a dark room.

In my book, *The Aware Baby,* I recommend that parents sleep with their baby. This practice of co-family sleeping can be extended into the preschool years if the parents have no objection to it. A common fear is that the child will never want to leave the parents' room, but most children do eventually want to have a room of their own. If you think that your child is ready to move into a separate room at night, you can prepare a little bed in another room, and suggest that he sleep there. Even though your child may like the idea and be willing to go to sleep there, do not be surprised if he wanders back to your bed in the middle of the night:

> Sarah slept next to me in my bed from the day she was born. As she grew older, she slept on a crib mattress next to our mattress (on the floor). At three-and-a-half years of age, she requested sleeping in the same room as her brother (who was eight years old). At first she came back to my bed in the middle of every night, but eventually began staying in her own bed all night long. Then, when she was just four years old, I was suddenly hospitalized for an emergency surgical operation. When I returned from the hospital, she began coming back to my bed each night. This lasted for several months before she began sleeping through the night in her own bed again. Then, when she was four-and-a-half years old, she started nursery school and once again began coming to my bed each night. At five years of age she was delighted at getting a room of her own and happily went to sleep in her own room. However, she still needed somebody to be with her until she fell asleep, and she still sometimes came to my bed in the middle of the night to finish the night close to me.

This example illustrates how the switch from dependency to independence occurs sporadically and is affected by external events. Every time there was a source of stress in my daughter's life, she felt the need for nighttime closeness.

Not only fears can cause a resistance to being alone, but also any accumulated painful feelings. Most babies need to cry every evening before falling asleep, and this need to release tensions by crying at bedtime continues for many children well into the preschool years. Young children may find a pretext to allow themselves to begin crying. Their favorite pajamas are in the laundry, you bought the wrong kind of tooth paste, and so on. It is not necessary to "fix" things or cater to their every demand when you suspect that there are some underlying feelings of frustration that need to be expressed. Instead, the crying and raging can be accepted and encouraged.

Sometimes children do not cry spontaneously but become hyperactive and "wound up" at bedtime. This shows itself by frantic (and often unacceptable) activity that tends to increase, rather than decrease, as the child becomes more tired. This is usually an indication of a need to cry and rage. Sometimes setting a physical limit helps the crying get started. You can take your child to the bathroom with you, close the door and stay there with him. Or you can try holding your child firmly to stop the frantic movements. This will help him channel his tensions into crying instead of hyperactivity. If you let your child alone, he may eventually find a way of crying on his own, sometimes by "accidentally" hurting himself or by provoking a sibling to hurt him. Once such a child has had a good cry, he will become relaxed, calm, and able to go to sleep.

Naptimes can also be a source of problems, which can be dealt with in similar ways: providing closeness and encouraging a release of feelings. Although it may be convenient for parents to have their children take naps in the afternoon, not all young children need them. Individual sleep needs vary greatly. Hereditary factors, rate of growth, health, and amount of exercise all play a role in determining how much sleep a child needs. An additional factor is the amount of crying: those who are allowed to cry enough seem to require less sleep than those whose feelings are more repressed. (Both of my children stopped taking naps soon after their second birthdays.) If your child is ready to give up naps, it does little good to try to force him to sleep during the day.

Exercises

Explore your childhood.

1. Were you punished as a child? How? Recall a few specific incidents and talk about how you felt. Were you ever given rewards for "good" behavior? How did it make you feel?

2. Were you expected to obey your parents' commands without questioning? If so, how did you feel about this?

3. What memories do you have from your childhood about household chores and about bedtime? Express your feelings. Do you wish your parents had acted any differently?

Express your feelings about your child.

1. Make a list of the major conflicts you have with your child. How do you feel about each one? What do you feel like doing to your child at those times? (This is not necessarily what you *should* do!)

2. Do you frequently lose patience with your child and hit or yell? How do you feel afterwards?

3. How do you feel when your child acts obnoxiously, uncooperatively, or generally "bratty?"

Nurture yourself.

1. Are your basic needs being filled (for food, rest, recreation, etc.?) If not, what can you do to obtain the help you need and to take care of yourself?

2. Are you involved with an authoritarian boss in your work situation, or an abusive spouse at home? If so, how does this make you feel? How can you work together to improve the situation?

3. Are you feeling the effects of current oppression or stereotyping in your life (for being a woman, black, Jewish, poor, physically handicapped, etc.)? If so, take steps to find the kind of emotional support that will help you feel good about yourself and give you the courage to confront the oppressive attitudes of others towards you.

CHAPTER 6: FRIENDS AND FOES

Children's relationships with other people are discussed in this chapter. One of the tasks of early childhood is to learn to get along with others. Families provide excellent training grounds for this because the constant encounters with siblings and their needs provide the experiences necessary for developing social skills. There is bound to be some arguing and fighting even in the healthiest of families, as children learn to share and think about other people's needs. The manner in which sibling conflicts are handled can have a profound effect on children's later interpersonal relationships.

The sexual abuse of young children is also addressed in this chapter. It is becoming clear that sexual abuse is much more prevalent than was previously believed. Every family needs to be aware of protecting children from this. A final section deals with children's relationships with stepparents.

How Can I Prepare My Child for a New Baby?

It is important to prepare children for the birth of a younger sibling. Depending on the age of the child, this can be done with books, pictures, doll play, or simply talking about the coming event. If the child is old enough to ask questions, there are likely to be lots of them, and these need to be answered in a straightforward manner. It is important to avoid giving the impression that the older child will now have a little sister or brother to "play with." This will only lead to disappointments when the child discovers how little the new baby can do. The parents can mention instead that the new baby will be quite helpless and will need to be taken care of.

The child's questions can lead to such topics as where the baby came from or how it started growing, and this may be a perfect time to introduce basic concepts of human sexuality and reproduction. It is important, however, not to give any more information than the child needs at the moment, or is ready to assimilate.

As the due date approaches, the child will probably want to know exactly what will happen: how and when the baby will come out, where the mother will be, where he will be, who will take care of him, and so on. This all needs to be explained several times, and perhaps even rehearsed. There is always a great deal of uncertainty surrounding birth: the sex of the baby, the day and time of birth, even the possibility of an emergency Cesarean. It is better to explain the nature of the uncertainties, rather than give your child information that may prove to be false. You can tell your child that there are some things nobody knows ahead of time.

As I mentioned in Chapter 3, many families are now allowing their children to be present at the birth of a sibling (Simkin, 1987). If you plan to have your child present at the birth, then certain additional preparations are recommended. He needs to know all about labor and the stages of labor, and he should be told exactly what will be expected of him. Also, in order to avoid possible disappointments, it is a good idea to explain everything that will happen, as well as everything that *could* happen. Do not leave out descriptions of bleeding, and the birth of the placenta. The birth itself can be rehearsed with the child present, so that he knows what to expect. He needs to be forewarned that his mother will be very busy and not available to respond to his needs, hold him, or even speak to him during labor and birth. He also needs reassurance that his mother may make unusual sounds and be in unusual positions, but that this does not imply she is ill. I recommend having an adult available whose sole job during the birth experience is to pay attention to your child.

Once these preparations have been taken, witnessing the birth can be a wonderful experience for your child, both emotionally and intellectually. Allowing your older child to be a part of the birth can allow him to begin bonding with his sibling right from the start. Anyone who witnesses a birth tends to be more bonded to the baby than people who are not present (Klaus & Kennell, 1976). The sight of blood or of his mother in pain will not frighten a child if he has been properly prepared for the event. Our culture tends to shield children from intense experiences such as birth and death, but there is no reason to do so. Children can handle these events perfectly well, provided someone is available to answer their questions and be attentive to and accepting of their feelings. My son was present at the birth of my daughter:

Nicky was 4 years and 11 months old when his sister, Sarah, was born. All throughout my pregnancy he asked many questions, and we borrowed books from the library that described the growth of a baby and the birth process. As my due date approached, Nicky was present when my husband and I rehearsed the various stages of labor and the breathing techniques. He was told all about the birth process, but we also informed him that sometimes doctors have to cut a woman's abdomen to take the baby out. (I did not want Nicky to be disappointed or confused if I were to have an emergency Cesarean.) We agreed on a signal for him to be quiet: putting my right index finger up in the air would indicate the beginning of a contraction. This signal was rehearsed until he knew it well. The birth was to take place in a hospital that allowed families to be present. My mother was prepared to be with Nicky throughout the birth: to bring him to the hospital and keep him occupied if he got bored. The birth went smoothly. Nicky was very attentive and interested, obeyed my signals perfectly, and was not in the least frightened by the sight of blood. He enjoyed conversing with the doctor and asked many questions. He was allowed to hold his baby sister before she was one hour old. Right from the start, he was extremely attached to her, wanting to hold her frequently, and even wishing she could sleep in his room! He took a great interest in her growth and development and felt responsible for her safety and well-being. I am convinced that his presence at her birth helped create this strong bond between them. Although he did experience strong jealousy and antagonism at times, as she grew older, he never tried to harm her.

What Can Be Done About a Child's Resentment of a New Baby?

After a child has been an only child for several years, with both parents available to give her attention when she needs it, the birth of a baby is an extremely difficult adjustment. It is as if a man said to his wife, "Honey, I love you so much, but I want to have another wife like you, so I'm going to bring one home soon, and then we will all live happily together. I hope you will love my new wife. She can keep you company, and the two of you will be able to do fun things together." How would you feel? (If you are a man, imagine your wife saying she plans to bring home another husband.)

Even when all possible preparations and precautions are taken, resentment and anger towards a new baby can occur and can manifest itself in most disagreeable ways, particularly by acts of aggression towards the baby or the parents. Other manifestions of a child's distress include uncooperative or demanding behavior and regression to more infantile modes of behavior. After the new baby is born, an older child may refuse to feed or dress herself, or begin soiling or wetting her pants after having used a toilet for months. Night awakenings can also increase. Some may request to nurse or use a bottle again, even though they may be well past that stage.

When children show these signs of distress, the situation can become exasperating for the parents, who have not only a new baby to care for, but also an older "problem child." Scoldings, spankings, or isolation only make the problem worse because the child is already feeling insecure and anxious. She is not sure of being loved and feels very threatened by the baby.

The child's two needs at the moment are 1) the need for love and reassurance, and 2) the need to release feelings of resentment and anger. The first need can be filled by giving your child individual attention. Try to set aside some time each day, even if only ten or fifteen minutes, when you devote your attention entirely to your older child, and do whatever she wants to do. Depending on her age, she may want to play a game, cuddle, or use this time with you to pretend to be a baby. Whatever she asks for is what she needs from you. You can show her pictures of her as a baby, and tell her about her birth and things she did as a baby.

The need to release feelings of resentment and anger can be filled by allowing and accepting crying and raging, as described elsewhere in this book. The slightest pretext may trigger a temper tantrum, and these outbursts need to be accepted. The following example illustrates intense raging in my son that was triggered by jealousy:

> At six-and-a-half years of age, Nicky's jealousy of Sarah reached a peak, probably because his grandmother (who usually gave him a lot of attention) was gone for the summer. He became clingy and wanted to cuddle with me, especially when I was holding Sarah. One day, after I had spent an hour reading to him, he accidentally bumped his head and started crying. Just then, Sarah woke up. I picked her up and began to nurse her. This was just too much for Nicky, who screamed at the top of his voice, "I don't *want* you to hold Sarah!" He screamed and cried and started to kick at me. The crying was acceptable to me, but the kicking was not, so I went with Sarah to another room and closed the door while Nicky cried outside the door. After he promised not to kick me, I opened the door and let him in. He continued to cry, and after Sarah had finished nursing, he crawled into my lap to finish his sobbing. Afterwards he was in a great mood and played quite happily by himself.

Play-fighting can also be very useful in helping children express anger and resentment. The following example from a mother I interviewed illustrates the use of playful wrestling and laughter to help a child release feelings of anger about a baby sibling:

> It started when Jimmy was over two years old, and Nancy was five or six months old. He would start hitting me when I was

nursing her, or else tear things apart, so that I could not sit and nurse her peacefully. He wanted my attention. It was very obvious. One day, when he was acting this way, as soon as I was able to give him attention, I wrestled with him, and made it playful and fun. He would push against me with all his strength, and I would let him "win." He did lots of laughing. We did this for maybe half an hour. He loved it! Then, he just relaxed and leaned on me and said, "Mommy, I love you." It was incredible! He's not usually that demonstrative about his love.

If your child purposely attempts to hurt the baby, this behavior must be stopped immediately. The best way to accomplish this without making your child feel rejected is to hold your child, and with the use of gentle but firm restraint, keep her in your arms, away from the baby. The child is likely to begin crying and raging as soon as her aggressive act is interrupted in this manner. This does not imply that you are hurting your child. On the contrary, you are giving her the opportunity to discharge her feelings of anger. She may protest vigorously and try to get away, but firm, continued holding may be necessary at times like these (as described in Chapter 5). You can explain that you have to keep holding her so she will not hurt the baby. Let her go after a while to observe her behavior, and if she acts aggressively towards the baby again, you can hold her some more. It is important that this holding be done in a spirit of love and not as punishment or revenge. Once her rage has passed, she will be much relieved and also much more loving towards the baby.

If your child expresses her feelings verbally, these too need to be accepted. Outbursts such as "I hate you," or "I hate my baby brother," are best accepted rather than denied or scolded. Because it is so painful to parents to see one of their children hate another, it is tempting to say, "You don't really hate him," or "I don't want to hear such things." A more helpful response would be, "I understand how you feel. It must be very hard for you right now, with this baby around all the time. I bet you wish he would go right back where he came from, and then we could be together just the two of us again, the way we used to be." With such a response, a child will feel truly understood, with her feelings acknowledged and accepted.

Doll play can also be very helpful in allowing both boys and girls to express their feelings towards a new baby. When the baby is born, you can give your older child a doll. Do not be surprised if she loves and cuddles the doll one day, but hits it or throws it on the floor the next day. This is an important outlet for her feelings, and hitting the doll may help prevent her from hitting the real baby. When your child is showing aggression towards the new baby, you can give her the doll and ask her to show you what she feels like doing. Make it clear that she cannot hit the baby, but she may take her feelings out on the doll.

Child-rearing techniques that rely on behavior modification are especially deceptive when used in this type of situation. It is possible, with the persistent use of rewards or punishments, to get a child to act *as if* she likes her baby sister or brother, but her underlying feelings will not have been dealt with at all, and she will still be full of anger and resentment. These feelings will continue to simmer until they have an outlet. If they are not allowed to be expressed harmlessly through play, laughter, tears, and tantrums, they may cause the child to be hurtful towards other children or animals, or even continue harming her sibling in devious ways when the parents are not looking. Although it is tempting to punish a child when she hits you or the baby, or reward her with candy when she behaves "nicely," this will not solve the underlying problem.

Why Do Siblings Fight with Each Other, and What Can Be Done About This?

One reason siblings fight is that they have chronic feelings of resentment towards each other. The more children there are in a family, the more likely they are to compete for parental attention and recognition (unless some siblings are old enough to help nurture younger ones). It is extremely difficult for two parents to give adequate attention on a daily basis to more than two children, and since children need a tremendous amount of one-to-one attention, very few ever get enough of it. During the hunter-gatherer stage of human evolution, it was common for aunts, uncles, and grandparents to live in close proximity to each other. Children had many adults they could interact with or even live with temporarily if there were conflicts in their immediate home environment. They also had other children to play with besides their siblings. Nowadays, nuclear families are often quite isolated, and children feel the need to compete for the attention of the one or two adults available.

Parents are often advised to stay out of their children's fights, because to intervene and give attention would only reinforce the fighting behavior. This is an oversimplification of the problem. There are times when children do fight for the sole purpose of gaining immediate parental attention, and to ignore the fighting may force the children to seek attention in other ways. But the underlying problem is still there: the children need more attention than they are getting. I recommend staying out of fights only if you are sure the children are simply trying to get your attention. You can then begin spending more time with them when they are not fighting in order to alleviate the problem.

It is important that each child in the family be given some individual attention on a daily basis. Also, each child needs some space he can call his own (even if it is one part of a room) as well as some toys that are exclusively his. This is necessary for a child's developing sense of individuality. Each child needs to feel that he is a special and valued member of the family, with his own unique interests and personality, and that he is loved and cherished as he is. It is helpful to find other adults to spend time with your children, especially if you are living far away from relatives.

There are several other reasons for sibling fights besides the need for immediate parental attention, and there are helpful ways of intervening in these situations. Another reason children fight is that they both want to play with the same toy but are not yet old enough to understand the concept of sharing or taking turns. Learning to share and take turns is difficult for very young children. They cannot easily see things from another person's perspective (Piaget, 1950) or infer what other people are thinking or feeling (Rubin & Everett, 1982). The ability to take other people's needs into account and find solutions to conflicts that are agreeable to everyone gradually increases during the pre-school years. This is learned through social interactions, but is also dependent on the maturation of the nervous system (Piaget, 1950). A four-year-old may stand between his parent and the television set without realizing that he is blocking his parent's view until this is pointed out to him. An eight-year-old is less likely to do this because he will spontaneously take his parent's perspective and needs into consideration.

If two children are fighting over a toy, parents can offer two major kinds of support: 1) encourage the children to release feelings by crying, and 2) help them communicate verbally with each other about the problem and arrive at a mutually agreeable solution. After listening to each child, you can say, "You two have a problem. John is upset because Karen keeps trying to take the fire engine away, and Karen is upset because she was playing with it first and wasn't yet done. You both want to play with the big fire engine at the same time. Can you think of a way to solve this problem?" This simple description of the problem is best done in a manner that does not accuse or take sides.

It may be necessary to be firm about not letting either child play with the toy until they can work out a solution that is agreeable to both of them. There are quite likely to be some tears along the way. When conflicts are handled this way, with crying allowed, and with no solution imposed from the outside, children usually do end up agreeing on a solution, and it is often a very creative one that the parents would never have thought of.

When parents impose a solution in an authoritarian manner, this deprives children of an opportunity to think about another person's needs and learn conflict-resolution skills. Parental solutions are usually not satisfactory anyway, and one or both of the children will feel cheated. Several examples of helping siblings reach their own mutually agreeable solutions are given in the book *Siblings Without Rivalry* (Faber & Mazlish, 1987).

Another reason for fights occurs when a younger child is feeling frustrated at not being able to do what an older sibling is doing. The following example of my own children illustrates this:

Nicky (age 7) enjoyed playing the piano and learning simple tunes. However, whenever he sat down at the piano and started to play, Sarah (age 2) also went to the piano and banged on the keys. I refrained from intervening to see if they could solve this problem by themselves. Nicky came up with several ingenious plans, such as giving her turns, playing pieces she could sing along with, finding something else for her to do, but all to no avail. She still bothered him when he played, and he would end up yelling at her. I felt that my assistance was needed. It looked to me as if Sarah was not thinking well about how to act, probably because of feelings of frustration at not yet being able to play the piano. The next time she bothered him, I held her, lovingly but firmly, to prevent her from bothering Nicky. She cried hard in my arms, and afterwards did not bother him any more, but played happily by herself while he practiced. However, the problem would periodically return, even though I encouraged her to cry on several occasions. I then decided to try spending time with her at the piano when Nicky was not playing it, to help her learn to play. With my attention, she began to make up little tunes at the piano. Once she realized that she, too, was able to "play the piano," she hardly ever bothered him when he played.

In this example, the frustrations kept recurring until the younger child had acquired similar skills. Frustrations like these are inevitable because children naturally want to learn to do everything they see others doing.

Any time a younger sibling is excluded from an activity, a fight is likely to occur. Parents can be helpful at such times by providing a means by which the younger child can participate at his own level of competence, if possible. This will help to minimize antagonism between the siblings. If Dad and big brother are baking a birthday cake for Mother, little sister can help by stirring, dumping in the flour, or greasing the pans.

However, when older siblings are playing with their peers, they are not always going to want to include their little sisters or brothers in their activities, and should not be made to do so. It is not our job as parents always to make things perfect for our children. When parents insist that the younger ones be included it usually does not work out at all and nobody has any fun. The most helpful approach is to acknowledge the younger child's feelings and encourage a release of anger and frustration.

There is an additional reason for sibling fights that is possibly the most common one, but also the most unrecognized. Fights are often a means by which children communicate to their parents that something is bothering them, and children often fight with each other so they can have a pretext for releasing pent-up feelings. They deliberately choose to use each other in this manner. A boy who has been teased at school may come home and purposely pick a fight with his brother so that his brother will hit him. This will then furnish him with a pretext for crying.

Sibling fights that lead to tears can thus be considered in many cases productive opportunities for discharging painful feelings. Strange as it may seem, when siblings continually choose to upset each other to the point of tears, they are probably benefitting from the crying that occurs. Parents can be helpful in these cases by accepting the crying. A mother I interviewed reported this about her five-year-old son and three-year-old daughter:

> They scream a lot at each other. They get angry about all kinds of things. She gets so frustrated when he teases her. A lot of the rivalry is over toys that they both want to play with at the same time. But when Greg was away for a week, Julie still cried a lot. She continued to have temper tantrums even when everything was revolving totally around her and her needs. She would throw herself on the middle of the kitchen floor and scream. It definitely showed me that she just needed to have them. She had to get her daily quota of crying!

If children fight to the point of inflicting serious harm on each other, immediate intervention is necessary. It may be necessary to separate the children physically by stepping in between them or by firmly holding the one who is about to hit the other. Parents can then acknowledge the children's feelings. Usually this will be sufficient to allow the would-be aggressor to feel his feelings, rather than act them out, and to begin crying rather than continue hitting. The goal is to stop the violence, but not necessarily the noise. Loud crying may be exactly what is needed at the time.

It is also important to intervene when one child is consistently being teased or taken advantage of. It is not fair to let a child be hurt repeatedly in this manner by a sibling. The child who is acting hurtfully needs to be stopped and assisted in expressing his feelings. It is also helpful to sit with the child at a time when he is not picking on his sibling, and discuss the ongoing problem. If this is done in a non-blaming, supportive way, the child may mention something that will help explain the situation. Perhaps, without realizing it, the parents have been favoring one child, or perhaps one child has been excelling in some area that makes his sibling feel inferior and insecure. Chronic teasing, criticisms, or inter-ruptions of one sibling by another can become a habit-pattern resulting from non-specific jealousy and feelings of insecurity. A light, humorous interruption can greatly help to reduce the behavior and allow for a release of tensions through laughter. Here is a description of one family's solution:

> Jerry (age 5) used to tease Heather (age 3) a lot. He would say "doo doo head" to her, and "diddle dee, diddle dee" just to irritate her. After I discussed this with him, he realized that it was just a bad habit, and I said I would help him stop. We agreed that every time he started saying these little things to her, I'd say, "Canteloupes, Jerry!" (and Heather has added "Strawberries!"). It's really worked well, because he would stop teasing her whenever we said this, and he would actually laugh about it. We didn't have to say "Jerry, don't do that, you shouldn't do that." We didn't have to go through all that put-down of him. He seemed to appreciate that, even when Heather said it, we were reminding him that he just had that habit, and were helping him stop it. He didn't feel that we were mad at him or blaming him for it.

There is one additional factor involved in sibling fights which stems more from a general attitude about competitiveness in our culture than from any immediate cause. In Chapter 4 I described the high level of competitiveness in many industrialized nations, and how it affects children in their play. These competitive values also contribute to sibling rivalry.

One way these values are transmitted to children is in the tendency to push them to accomplish tasks at an early age, as described in the book *The Hurried Child* (Elkind, 1981). This is the logical result of a competitive culture, and many parents feel under pressure to get their children to read, write, be mathematical geniuses, or play musical instruments at an early age. Independence is also considered to be a virtue. Children are affected by their parents' anxiety about their growth, and any development that is considered to be slow is likely to be the source of tension and concern for the entire family. All of these factors can contribute to sibling rivalry because they make children feel insecure about their abilities and skills.

We can do our best to resist the pull to get our children to succeed and perform at an early age. This will not be easy because the entire culture makes us feel that "earlier is better." We can also try to make our homes less competitive by eliminating all comparisons of each other. This may be more difficult than we think. It is very tempting to compare children to each other. Words come out of our mouths before we realize what we are saying: "Why aren't you ready for school yet? Susan is always dressed on time." "Matthew is our artist, and Mary is our little dancer."

When we compare children to each other or put them in roles according to what they do well, we unintentionally hurt them. What if Matthew secretly yearns to dance but doesn't dare try because his little sister receives all the praise and encouragement? Furthermore, if one child is labeled slow or messy compared with his siblings, he may continue to act that way because that is how his parents see him. He may even attempt to excel at being slow or messy if his achievements in other areas are not recognized. Furthermore, such labeling cannot help but lead to resentments, which will surface as antagonism and fighting between the siblings.

Children who are exposed to competitive values naturally tend to be anxious and angry when one of their siblings receives more time, attention, or gifts. Because of this tendency to compare amounts received, parents sometimes make huge efforts to give equally to all their children. This is not necessary. Children do not have to receive exactly the same number of gifts or precisely the same number of minutes of attention from their parents. Instead of trying to keep score, a more helpful approach is to focus on giving according to each child's individual needs: "Michelle needed new shoes today, and when you need new shoes I'll buy some for you." If the parents minimize the tendency to give equally, the children will (hopefully) compare themselves less with their siblings and realize that each of them will receive according to their own individual needs (Faber & Mazlish, 1987).

To conclude, there are several factors that can cause siblings to fight with each other: feelings of resentment and jealousy, the need for attention, the inability to understand another person's point of view, frustration at being less skillful than a sibling, feelings of exclusion, the need to release pent-up feelings, and general competitiveness. Parents can be quite helpful, both in preventing conflicts and in helping children deal with them when they occur.

How Can I Remain Objective When My Children Fight?

Most parents find their children's arguments and fights extremely disagreeable and annoying. It is painful to see their well-loved children angry at each other. Because of these feelings and the desire to have a peaceful home, it is sometimes tempting to impose a ready-made solution that will, hopefully, make everybody happy. It is also tempting to take sides and blame or defend one of the children. Such interventions are usually not helpful, especially since the real issue is not always what it appears to be.

Some parents find their children's fights so intolerable that they resort to yelling, hitting, or punishments. This, of course, only gives the children a model for the very behavior the parents are attempting to stop. It shows the children that conflicts are to be solved through violence, and it teaches them that the person with the most power is always the winner. The child who is hit or yelled at becomes hurt. If these feelings are not released, they may cause the child to act hurtfully towards others in similar ways.

Many parents find it difficult to remain calm and objective when their children are fighting because the parents are feeling that they have failed in some way. Also, sibling fights can trigger memories of their own fights with siblings when they were younger. Perhaps there is unresolved anger at an older sibling or guilt at having mistreated a younger one. If their own parents fought frequently, any fighting in a home can bring up feelings of terror and a compulsive desire to end the argument at any cost. Here is what a father said to me about his feelings when his three-year-old daughter hit her baby sister:

> When Nancy hits Sandra I see red. I get angry, and I feel like hitting. I know it's not good, but that's what I feel like doing. It's the first impulse. Or I shout, and that's not good either. I've been trying to learn to stay calm and listen empathically and all that. I'm a counselor, I ought to be able to do that, but I just get emotional when I see one of my kids hurt by another one of my kids. It's hard for me to control myself. I think it brings back memories of my childhood, of my older sister who used to beat up on me and then get away with it by telling Mom or Dad that I had started it. I still have scars on my arms where my sister scratched and bit me.

If you find yourself acting inappropriately when your children fight, and would like to change your response, a first step is to explore feelings from your own past experiences involving fighting and violence and release these painful feelings by laughing, crying, and raging (preferably with a supportive and objective listener, if you can find one). Once your feelings are expressed, you will find it easier to remain calm and objective when your own children fight with each other. You can then deal with the situation creatively and more effectively.

How Can I Help My Child Learn to Get Along with Friends?

Children experiment with different ways of acting towards others, and this is one way they learn about other people's feelings and the effects of their own behavior. They are not born knowing that other children do not like having toys taken away from them or do not like being told what to do. This has to be learned.

Young children are not always tactful and sometimes make blunt statements to each other. It is not uncommon to hear them say, "I hate you," "You're mean," or "I'm not your friend any more." Five minutes later, they may be playing happily together again! These rash statements are children's way of expressing the momentary, but intense, feelings of anger or irritation with each other. There is no need to intervene or to make an issue of such interactions.

When a disagreement arises during play, you can be a helpful mediator if the children do not seem to be able to solve the problem by themselves:

> Sarah (age 6) and Helen (age 5) were playing dolls one day when I heard them crying and screaming at each other. This was unusual, so I went to see what was happening. They each had a different idea of what a specific doll should wear to a doll party they were planning. This was obviously an important issue for them and they had not been able to reach a solution. After giving each of them a chance to talk, I reflected back each girl's feelings: "Sarah, you want her to wear the green outfit because it is perfect for a hot day, and Helen, you want the white outfit because the green one is not fancy enough for a party. Can you two think of a solution that you will both be happy with?" Helen said, "We can't agree because we each want something different," and started to dress the doll in the white dress. Sarah grabbed the doll from her and there was more screaming and crying. Then I tried suggesting solutions, but all of my ideas were rejected. Finally I said, "I'm going to let you two work this out by yourselves. I think you can find a solution that you will both be happy with." I left them alone for a few minutes and heard no more screaming. When I went back

to them they showed me the doll who was wearing both outfits at once (something I never would have thought of)! They were both happy with this solution and seemed proud at having solved their conflict.

Hitting and biting are usually an indication of painful feelings (as is the case when this occurs between siblings). The child who frequently hits others is feeling insecure, hurt, angry, or scared, and needs help in expressing his feelings in ways that do not hurt other people. Allowing such a child the freedom of tears and harmless tantrums will help greatly to alleviate the problem. A nursery school teacher I interviewed described his approach with children fighting:

> At school very often children will be fighting over a toy, and if they're both holding onto a toy and struggling with it for a few seconds, the next move on a lot of children's part is to bite or to hit to get that toy. If I am there close enough, I just reach in between them, put my hand between them, and say "No." Or sometimes, when the child is just ready to strike the blow, or has his mouth open and his teeth poised over the other child's ear lobe or wrist, I just grab him gently and restrain him from going any further. Then flood gates open and tears just pour out. All of that intensity and all of that emotion at the moment are released just because of that restraint, that one simple restraint (either saying no or just holding him back). And that will often lead into a long crying session. There is usually no trace of aggression after the child has cried.

An only child may have difficulty at first interacting with peers, especially if he is used to a lot of attention from his parents during play. He may expect his friends to adopt whatever role he tells them to because he is used to his parents playing along with him in this manner. This will be interpreted by his friends as bossiness. An only child may also have difficulty with frankness and teasing from peers and with rough-and-tumble play because of lack of experience with this kind of interaction. These are not necessarily serious problems, and they can usually be overcome by repeated play experiences with other children.

How Can I Protect My Child from Sexual Abuse?

A survey found that almost one out of five female college students reported having been sexually abused in some way before the age of thirteen (Finkelhor, 1979). Evidence indicates that the sexual abuse of children is a widespread reality and has been happening for hundreds of years (Rush, 1980). In recent years a new awareness and understanding of sexual abuse has been developing. Because of this, people are less likely to keep it a secret.

An important factor in resisting sexual assault is to help children feel respected and powerful. If a child has been treated with respect from birth and not manipulated with either rewards or punishments or made to feel guilty for her behavior, she is more likely to have the courage to say "no" to an adult who is acting hurtfully or inappropriately towards her. Children who have been taught to obey blindly, without questioning authority, in a home where punishment is used, may be less able to resist sexual assault, and less likely to tell their parents about it because of a fear of consequences.

Information sharing is also very important. Children need to be warned about human irrationality and hurtful behavior because they are naturally trusting of everybody. You can inform your child that some adults do not treat children well and do mean things or touch private parts of their body, and that it is okay to say "no," go away, and tell someone about what happened.

Children often have the incorrect notion that "bad" people are easy to spot because they look evil. This notion may be due to books or television. Whatever the source, it is important to let children know that adults who look just like Mommy or Daddy can hurt them, and that even people they know and trust can treat them abusively. The message should be that adults (even their own parents) are not perfect and sometimes do hurtful things.

Discussion need not be limited to sexual abuse. Anytime you hear about or observe an adult treating a child with less than total respect, you can point this out to your own children. When we parents have the courage actually to interrupt oppression of other children, we can be powerful role models for our own children, who will then be more likely to stand up for themselves when an adult is abusing them.

If you feel uncomfortable leaving your child with someone because you have a "funny" feeling about the person, then *trust your own feelings,* even if he is a member of your own family. You can be particularly wary of men who describe little girls in sexual terms, such as: "She's got a lover's eyes," or "She would look good in a bikini." These are men who do not see children as children, but as potential sexual objects to fill their own needs. Be wary of daycare centers, schools, or classes that do not allow you to drop in and visit your child. If your child is invited to a friend's home, make sure you know the adults who will be responsible for her.

A good way to help children rehearse saying "no" is to play-act potential threatening scenes. The goal is to inform your children without making them feel too scared to be away from you. Information about sexual assault, as well as kidnapping, is best given cheerfully and matter-of-factly, just as you might teach your child how to cross a street without getting hit by a car.

If you yourself have been sexually abused, your own pain and fear can be transmitted to your children, who may then become overly fearful of strangers. Such a mistrust of people will limit their enjoyment of life. Any counseling or therapy you can obtain for yourself will benefit both you and your children.

If you are sexually attracted to your own children and are pulled to engage in sexual play with them, you need to see a therapist and get help. There is no need to feel guilty or to blame yourself for feelings such as these, because they originate in your own hurtful childhood.

Adult sex play with children is extremely confusing, frightening, and humiliating to children. Even very young ones are acutely aware of being taken advantage of when someone begins to touch them inappropriately. Victims of incest who were interviewed as adults reported having felt extremely ashamed and confused when their father (or other family member) touched them in inappropriate ways, even when this was done gently. They felt that they had no choice but to submit and tolerate the abuse. They also reported having felt unable, as children, to tell anybody, often because they were threatened with worse treatment if they told. Some felt that nobody would believe them or that they would be blamed. Others were afraid of disrupting the family or being put in a foster home (Armstrong, 1978).

Sexually abused children grow up with feelings of powerlessness and often a compulsion to be a victim in further abusive relationships, because of an inability to know the difference between being loved and being taken advantage of. Then, as parents, they compulsively try to re-enact what was done to them, taking on the abusive role with their trusting and innocent children as the victims.

This tragic cycle of abuse can be interrupted when adults become aware of and express their outrage at the cruel and humiliating things that were done to them. This requires a supportive and attentive listener who believes the adult and who can accept the expression of intense feelings of grief, anger, and fear.

What Can I Do if My Child Has Been Sexually Abused?

Any change in a child's behavior can be an indication of sexual abuse. This can include a regression in toileting habits, bedwetting, withdrawal, clinging behavior, sudden shyness or fearfulness, loss of appetite, nightmares or sleep disturbances, or resistance to going to school or playing with friends. The child may attempt to heal herself of the hurt by increased crying. If she does not feel safe enough to cry, she may resort to control patterns such as thumb sucking or clutching a favorite blanket or stuffed animal. More obvious clues might be a sudden preoccupation and interest in genitals (the child's own or other people's). This can include excessive masturbation, curiosity, or drawings of genitals. A sexually abused child may begin talking about sex acts or acting them out with dolls or friends in an attempt to understand what has happened. Signs of being uncomfortable with someone who was formerly trusted can be an indication of sexual assault.

If any of these symptoms occur without there being any obvious cause (such as the birth of a sibling, a move, or a divorce by the parents), then it is wise to investigate the possibility of sexual abuse.

If you discover that your child has indeed been sexually abused, it is extremely important to believe your child, to let her know she did the right thing by telling you, and to reassure her that nothing that happened was her fault. She also needs reassurance that you will protect her and take action so that it will not happen again.

The next step is to notify the police and seek help from a child abuse agency. It is important that the offender be confronted and legal action taken. This will be especially difficult for you and your child if the offender is a family member or close friend. You can let your child know that the goal is not to punish the person, but to make sure he gets the help he needs so he will not repeat the hurtful behavior with another child.

It is very important for you to express your own feelings, which may range from shock and disbelief to fear, guilt, or anger. You may need to cry and rage, but this is best done away from the child, who has her own feelings to deal with. Do not hesitate to seek the assistance of a professional counselor. You deserve all the help you can get.

Your child will also need to talk about the experience. This should be fully encouraged. If she tends to avoid the issue, it is probably because she does not feel safe enough, and may still be frightened of possible consequences. A competent therapist who has experience working with child sexual assault victims can be helpful. It is not a sign of weakness or failure to seek professional help when needed.

Are Young Children Sexually Attracted to Their Parents?

A major concept in psychoanalytic theory is the notion that young children normally become sexually attracted to the parent of the opposite sex and secretly desire to get rid of the other parent, so that they can have the desired love object all to themselves. This is referred to as the "Oedipus Complex" in boys, and the "Electra Complex" in girls. The outcome of this conflict is considered to have a central impact on future emotional adjustment. An inability to resolve this is supposed to be a major source of neurosis in adult life.

Evidence for this theory originally came from adults' reports of memories of sexual experiences with their parents. These were believed by Freud to be fantasies indicating the child's desire for such experiences, rather than actual memories of real happenings. This is a major component of Freud's drive theory. However, previous to Freud's drive theory, he had devised a theory (called the "seduction theory") in which he assumed that adults who came to him had various psychological problems because of early trauma, which often involved real sexual abuse by adults. His seduction theory was abandoned, however, because his contemporaries could not accept or admit the fact that adults could do such perverse things to children. The later drive theory, which replaced the seduction theory, discredited his patients' memories of early abuse by interpreting them as mere fantasies (Masson, 1984).

According to Alice Miller (1984), Freud's drive theory has served to perpetuate the oppression of children by failing to recognize the true source of psychological problems, which lies in early mistreatment and traumatic events. As mentioned previously, there is considerable evidence that the sexual abuse of young children is a widespread reality and that adults' memories of these events are accurate. The idea that children would want and choose to have sexual relations with an adult is not in accord with observations of children's behavior. Children normally have no understanding of or desire for sexual intercourse, as this urge arises only with the hormones of puberty.

When a young boy states that he will marry his mother some day, this is merely because she happens to be the most important woman in his life. The same can be said about a girl saying she will marry her father. Children who say these things have grasped the concept that people of opposite sexes get married, and they are simply expressing this understanding. It may also be a way of expressing the fact that they want a life-long relationship with their parents. Young children do not fully understand about relationships and generations, and they cannot imagine living with a stranger from outside the family, so they naturally assume that they will marry someone within the family. My daughter announced one day at three years of age that she would grow up and marry her grandfather! It would be a misunderstanding of what the child is saying to suggest that there is some deep, incestuous desire lurking under the innocent statement.

Instead of assuming that children harbor sexual desires and death wishes, we would be doing them a greater service if we focused on the way in which they get hurt and abused by those who have more power than they do. Any anger towards a parent of either sex is the result of having been hurt in some way by that parent. The sooner we can recognize this fact, the better we will be able to help our children develop into psychologically healthy adults.

Although children do not normally come to desire their parents sexually, this does not imply that they are without sexual feelings. Many children do masturbate, and some even discover how to have an orgasm before puberty. But this kind of sexual activity is of a personal and individual nature, being purely a pleasurable physical sensation. Children masturbate without any awareness that this has anything to do with sexual intercourse, reproduction, or being "in love." It can be an enjoyable act that is totally disassociated from any feeling of attachment or desire for another person. Children are not ready for interpersonal sexual contacts, and any child who felt free to do so would firmly reject all sexual overtures by adults.

What About Children's Sex Play with Each Other?

Young children sometimes like to play naked together and inspect each others' genitals. This usually takes the form of watching each other urinate or defecate or "playing doctor" together. This kind of play is usually accompanied by much giggling.

Children's sex play serves two major purposes. It is, first of all, a way for children to acquire information about human physiology and sex differences. Children naturally want to know all about their own and others' bodies, and how they differ from each other.

The second purpose of such play is a therapeutic one. Sex is a source of much embarrassment in many homes, and these feelings of shame are passed on from generation to generation. Children pick up on the fact that the sex organs are taboo subjects of conversation. There is great need for them to release their embarrassment and anxiety through the tension-release mechanism of laughter. This is why children laugh so much when playing naked together.

Children's sex play with each other is nothing to be concerned about, but parents may need to set some limits for purposes of safety and hygiene. Children should be told not to put any objects in their anuses and vaginas, and to wash their hands before and after touching themselves. This is normally a stage that children go through, and, once their curiosity is satisfied, they will not need to engage in such play. Attempts to ban such play will not stop it, but will only result in the children doing it secretly, and may even cause them to grow up feeling guilty or unable to fully accept themselves and their bodies.

Children who have been sexually abused may become overly interested in sex play with other children because they are attempting to understand what was done to them, and have a compulsive need to re-enact it with somebody else. This kind of behavior *can* be harmful to other children, especially if there is an imbalance of age or power. If this occurs, the child who is acting out the sexual distress needs therapy, so that he can be helped to release his feelings and so that other children will not be hurt. The child who was taken advantage of also needs help and support in expressing his feelings about what was done to him.

How Can I Help My Stepchild Adjust to Me?

Although it is not within the scope of this book to discuss all the issues involved in stepparenting, or in parenting after divorce, I would like to address one issue: that of helping a child adjust to a new parent.

Because of the frequency of divorces and remarriages, many parents today face the challenge of caring for a child who is not their own. This task is not easy. Most children are deeply affected by their parents' separation and have strong feelings of anger and guilt (Levitin, 1983). The period preceding the separation may have been one of extreme tension in the family and perhaps even violence, with little attention for the child. Anything you can do as a stepparent to help the child express his feelings will be beneficial in creating a warm, loving relationship between the two of you. Do not be surprised (and try not to take it personally) if your stepchild needs to express anger directly at you. An initial resentment of the new mother or father is common. A woman reported to me how she helped a three-year-old boy work through his anger at her:

> When I started living with Matthew and his son, Carl, the new living situation was difficult at first. Carl resented me being there instead of his mother and told me to go away repeatedly, in an angry tone of voice. The first few times he said this, I left him alone and went to my room, but after several days of hearing "Go away!" and "I hate you" every time he saw me, I realized I couldn't disappear from sight every time he was around. So one day I stayed in the living room and Carl came up to me pushing and shoving at my legs saying, "Go away, go away." I said, "No, I'm going to stay here." He pushed and yelled at me with intense anger, while his father sat close by. After a while we all sat on the floor with Carl between us pushing with all his strength at me with his arms, and at his father with his feet. He seemed to like the resistance. If we moved too far away, he scooted over so he could push at us again. I reassured Matthew that it was good for Carl to release his anger in this manner. This continued for over an hour, while Carl cried and yelled, "Go away, I hate you!" to each of us in

turn and pushed at us with his hands and feet. Finally I got tired and left. The next day, he started saying again, "I hate you" and began pushing at me, so his father and I spent another hour devoting our attention to him while he released his anger. It happened again a few times the following week, but after that he never again said that he hated me. We've become fast friends. Carl always runs to me and gives me a big hug when he sees me now!

Your own feelings toward a stepchild may not be immediately loving either, and there is no need to feel guilty if you are unable to love a stepchild as much as you would like to. If you have children of your own, it is only natural for you to feel more loving towards them. There is no point in saying that you love your stepchild as well as your own if you do not, because he will sense the insincerity of your words.

As with any parenting situation, it is important for you to be able to talk about your own feelings with an attentive listener and cry if you need to do so. The expression and release of your own resentments or annoyances will make it easier for you to treat all of your children well and avoid favoring one over the other.

How Are Children Affected by Parents' Fights?

Children of all ages are deeply affected when their parents argue and fight with each other. They feel anxious and guilty. The anxiety comes from seeing and hearing their parents act in ways that are irrational, hurtful, and violent. This is quite threatening to children, who rely on their parents for protection and love. The guilt stems from the fact that children often feel they are to blame for the fight, even when this is not the case (Ginott, 1965). The unpredictability of fights can cause chronic anxiety and wariness because children fear they could happen at any time.

Children sometimes take sides with one of the parents, especially if there is an ongoing conflict between the parents. This is not a healthy situation for the children, who need both parents to love and support them. When a child sides with one parent and rejects the other, this only deprives him of identifying with that parent and of learning important values and skills from him. Children may also learn to spy and gossip, and the parents may feel pushed to use bribes, flattery, or even lies in order to gain back the love of a child who has chosen to side with the other parent.

In order to help children deal with feelings resulting from parental fighting, it is important to give children attention as soon as possible after you are feeling calmer and the fight is over. Reassure your child that the two of you do love each other, and that you both love your child, and that sometimes you get so angry that you yell at each other. Give your child a chance to express his feelings, and acknowledge those feelings. Allow him to cry if he needs to or express how frightened he was. If your fighting is chronic and is having a negative impact on your children, it may be wise to see a marriage counselor or therapist.

Exercises

Explore your childhood.

1. How did you feel about your siblings? Did you fight or argue with siblings as a child? If so, how do you feel about the way this was handled by your parents?

2. Describe the earliest friend you remember having (outside of your family). What did you enjoy doing together? How did you feel with that friend?

3. Were you ever sexually abused? If so, have you had a chance to work through the feelings with a competent therapist?

Express your feelings about your child.

1. How do you feel about your child's ability to get along with siblings? If there are frequent conflicts, what do you feel like doing? (This is not necessarily what you *should* do!)

2. Does your child ever act bossy, aggressive, rude, or withdrawn around other children? How do you feel about that?

3. Are you fearful or mistrustful of other adults who care for your child? Do you have reason to believe that your child is being (or has been) sexually abused? How do you feel about that? How do you feel about giving your child information about sexual abuse?

Nurture yourself.

1. Make a new friend, or renew contact with an old friend.

2. Take steps to get closer to one of your siblings (or other family members). Is there something unsaid that you need to say to each other in order to improve your relationship?

3. Take the time with your spouse or partner to appreciate each other every day. If there is continual tension in your relationship with your spouse, take steps to begin seeing a marriage counselor or therapist.

CHAPTER 7: EATING AND AILMENTS

This chapter discusses ways that parents can help their children deal with the feelings surrounding food, doctors, hospitals, illness, and pain. It is not intended as a substitute for medical treatment. Parents are advised always to seek out the best medical care available in cases of accidents, illness, pain, or eating disorders.

Pain and disease are closely related to emotions. There is considerable evidence that people under emotional stress are more prone to illness. On the other hand, feelings such as grief, fear, anger, guilt, and confusion are often *caused* by sickness and pain.

In Western societies, this interrelationship between feelings and physical health is not usually addressed by the medical profession, which has been trained to focus primarily on the physical aspects of disease. Because of this, parents can play an important role by supplementing medical treatment of their children with a supportive environment that allows for full expression of children's feelings.

What Can I Do About Eating Problems?

During the early childhood years, eating habits are quite different from those of adults. Many young children are not satisfied with only three meals a day, are likely to go on food binges, and often have strong dislikes for specific foods. Parents often wonder how to deal with this.

Studies have shown that, when trusted and allowed to select their own foods, babies obtain a balanced and healthful diet (Davis, 1928). A self-selection feeding approach can be used from birth on (as described in my book, *The Aware Baby*). At first, the baby can be nursed on demand. When solid foods are introduced, the baby can be allowed to choose, from a small selection of foods, what and how much she wants to eat.

This same approach can be continued during the early child-hood years. An excellent book describing this approach to self-demand feeding is called *Are You Hungry?* (Hirschmann & Zaphiropoulos, 1985). Young children can be trusted to select a balanced diet, provided healthful foods are readily available at all times. Parents can prepare and serve regular meals during the day for themselves and their children, just as they would normally do, but if the children do not like what is being served, the only respectful approach is to ask the child what she would like to eat instead. There is no need to cook another meal. Instead, simple, healthful snack foods can be kept available (that require little or no preparation) so that young children can eat what they want.

In between mealtimes, the children can be free to help them-selves to these same snack foods at any time. If these foods include fruits, vegetables, grain products, and high protein foods, there will be no need to worry about the children obtaining a balanced diet, because their instinct for survival will cause them to eat those foods that their body needs and in proper quantities for maximum health.

When a visitor comes to stay in your home, you would probably attempt to have foods available that the guest enjoys eating, and you would not tell her what, when, or how much she must eat. You would certainly not make her finish everything on her plate, and if she comes to you one half hour before dinner is ready saying she is hungry, you would not tell her that she has to wait. Instead, you might offer her something you happen to have on hand, such as a piece of fruit, a cracker, or some cheese. There is no reason to treat children any differently from a respected guest who hap-pens to be sharing your home for several years.

Some children develop a strong distaste for certain foods and will refuse even to try a new food. They should not be made to do so. No amount of reasoning, cajoling, bribery, or trickery will make a child like a food she has developed an aversion to. There is really no reason that a child should be made to eat a specific food. Many children refuse any foods that are combined, such as in a casserole, but will eagerly eat the same foods served plainly and separately. Others develop a distaste for certain foods because of appearance or texture: pepper on food "looks dirty," parsley "tickles " and bread crusts are "too hard."

Other reasons for rejecting certain foods have to do with the child's current fears. If a child is afraid of toilets, any food that resembles feces may be rejected. Other foods may be particularly desirable because of their symbolic or play value. A slice of cheese may be preferred to a chunk of the same cheese, because the child may want to take bites out of the slice to create different animal shapes. A child who has a baby sibling may want to eat foods similar in texture to those the baby eats. There is no harm in catering to these preferences. If no big issue is made of these whims and aversions, children will eventually outgrow them and begin to eat a wider variety of foods quite spontaneously. In fact, children are much more likely to taste something new if no issue is made of it at all.

Many parents have been led to believe that children must eat three well-balanced meals every day, and not eat very much in between meals. Most adults do follow this eating pattern because work schedules are set up for this. Consequently, it is not unusual for adults to have to eat lunch at a specific time whether they are hungry or not, because it is their lunch hour. Many adults have lost touch with their body's signals of hunger and fullness because of having to eat for convenience and social reasons. Furthermore, we do not always take the time to think well about the kinds of foods we eat, and often eat foods that produce ill-health or digestive problems. Recent studies have found that one out of every five Americans weighs at least 20% more than the desired weight for height (American Institute for Cancer Research Newsletter, Winter 1988).

Young children are generally better in touch with their body's nutritional needs than are adults, especially if they have not yet had their natural eating preferences controlled and manipulated. Although it may be difficult to admit, your sporadic four-year-old eater may actually be obtaining optimal nutrition, while you yourself, with three "well-balanced" meals a day, may be obtaining either more or less than your body actually needs.

Children do go on food binges and prefer one kind of food for a few days. This is nothing to be concerned about. One day for dinner my five-year-old daughter wanted nothing but sweet potatoes, even though she was also offered meat loaf and creamed broccoli. Another day she wanted nothing but cheese. I realized that, in any given week, she actually obtained a varied and balanced diet containing adequate amounts of protein, carbohydrates, fats, and vitamins, and she kept herself very healthy on this unusual eating pattern.

If your child has health problems, it may not be wise to follow such a liberal self-demand feeding approach, and medical opinion is always recommended whenever your child has a weight or eating problem of any kind. These can be indications of illness.

A mother I interviewed reported how difficult it is for her to maintain a relaxed attitude about her daughter's eating habits:

> My self-esteem is directly linked to what Angie puts into her mouth. The other day she was looking for popsicles in the freezer, and she discovered some frozen vegetables in a bag, and said, "Let's have some of these." It was three o'clock in the afternoon, and I almost fell over from surprise. Of course I cooked them up and served them to her and she actually ate them! I felt that I had finally succeeded as a woman because my child actually ate something I prepared that was good for her. At other times, when she doesn't eat what I think is good for her or doesn't finish what's on her plate, I try very hard not to say anything, or to let on that it's important to me. But secretely I'm a wreck inside because she doesn't eat what I wish she would eat.

A somewhat different situation arises around eating issues when a child uses food as a pretext to do some crying. Children who are feeling a need for a good cry will often find a pretext that allows them to get started (see Chapter 1). When this need is felt at mealtimes, children typically become extremely demanding and overly critical of foods. These whims need not be catered to, because the children do not really want them to be. What children need at these times is a limit set, so that they can then have a valid pretext for crying. When nothing you do is "right," as far as your child is concerned, when you feel that her demands are becoming unreasonable, or if she is acting frantic and whiny, then it is quite appropriate simply to say, "no," to whatever the issue is at hand. "No, I'm not going to cut up your potato for you because you can do it yourself." This will probably allow your child to cry and rage, thereby releasing her pent-up feelings.

Some parents try to cater to every single whim in a well-intentioned attempt to fill their child's needs, not realizing that these whims are often not genuine needs at all. If every unreasonable whim is catered to in this kind of situation, you will become exhausted and resentful, your child will not have an opportunity to discharge her feelings, and she will continue to be quite difficult to live with. Or you may find you have a bigger problem to deal with, as the following example illustrates:

> Two-year-old Willie woke up whiny and fussy. At breakfast he wanted milk on his cereal, so his mother poured some milk on it. Then he complained because he wanted milk to drink in a glass. Since there was no milk left, his mother poured some of the milk from the cereal into a glass for him. He poured it back into his cereal dish, but then complained again that he wanted milk to drink. His mother patiently poured some milk back into his glass. He then picked up the glass, looked at his mother and calmly and deliberately poured the milk onto the floor. He then began crying because he did not have any milk to drink!

In this example, the child obviously needed to cry (he was whiny to begin with), but he required a reason to help him get started. His mother unintentionally prevented him from having a pretext to cry because she kept giving into his whims. So he deliberately set up a situation that was impossible for his mother to "fix." The spilled milk could have been prevented if the mother had said earlier that there was no milk for him to drink. At that point, he probably would have begun the crying that he needed to do.

It may be tempting, during such situations, to resort to punishment because the child's behavior can be so exasperating. Children do not do these things out of spite or "naughtiness" or with an intent to make life hard for their parents. They act this way because they need to release feelings. If authoritarian and punitive methods are used at these times (such as a spanking or sending a child to her room), this will probably allow a pretext for crying, and the child will finally release her tears. However, this healing will occur at a cost to the child's self-esteem and to her relationship with her parents because it will result in a new hurt: that of being misunderstood and punished.

What If My Child Uses Food to Suppress Feelings?

The self-demand approach to feeding described above works best when combined with the other suggestions in this book, specifically those regarding children's expressions of feelings. When the need to cry is misunderstood during infancy, parents often try to stop the crying by means of nursing or feeding their baby. Only some crying indicates a need to be fed. Babies also need to spend time crying about emotional hurts and frustrations in order to release tensions and heal themselves. This kind of crying is best handled by holding the baby without feeding or distracting him from his feelings.

If a child's crying was repeatedly stopped by means of nursing or food during infancy, then he is likely to develop a control pattern involving food: he will tend to want to eat something whenever he is feeling upset for any reason: frustration, boredom, fear, sadness, confusion, or even physical pain or fatigue. Since he has not learned to express his feelings by crying and raging, he will tend to repeat whatever distraction was used to get him to stop crying. If food was the distraction used, such a child will think he is hungry when in fact he is really emotionally upset. He will become addicted to eating, just as a smoker becomes addicted to cigarettes in an attempt to repress painful feelings.

It is not always easy to tell if a child is using food to suppress feelings, and you may have difficulty deciding whether or not to intervene. If your child is overweight, and no medical cause has been discerned, then it is quite likely that eating is his way of suppressing feelings.

It is never too late to help such a child. The remedy for this kind of situation is to make your child's home environment more accepting of the expression of feelings. If your child reaches for one cookie after another, you can gently stop him and say, "Do you really want a cookie now? Or would you prefer to cuddle with me and talk? Is there something upsetting you that I can help you with?" You can also encourage and accept crying at other times (as described in Chapter 1).

If this approach does not work, and your child continues to binge on certain foods to the detriment of his health, you may need to intervene more actively by limiting those foods. This is quite likely to cause your child to cry and rage, and this reaction is to be expected. He is beginning to release the feelings that his eating control pattern has prevented him from expressing.

What About Candy?

Many parents wonder how much candy and other sweet foods to allow their children to eat, and they fear that, if allowed all the candy they wanted, children would eat nothing else, become ill or overweight, and ruin their teeth.

There are two reasons that children sometimes find it hard to think clearly about candy and do tend to eat quantities that are detrimental to their health. The first reason was described in the previous section. When a child's crying is repeatedly stopped during infancy by being nursed, she becomes accustomed to having something sweet in her mouth every time she is feeling upset. This kind of control pattern can become further well-established if parents give candy in situations of stress, such as a medical procedure, during times of waiting and boredom, or when the child is scared, tired, or sad. Any time a child eats something sweet when she is experiencing painful feelings, her feelings will be temporarily repressed, instead of released, and the tendency to want sugar the next time she is feeling upset will be even more strongly reinforced.

Many adults secretly binge on sweets when they are depressed, lonely, or frustrated with their lives. This kind of eating pattern is easily passed on to children, who learn to reach for the candy box when they are bored or upset. If your child is addicted to sweets you may need to limit her consumption of them and encourage her to cry and rage rather than repress her feelings by eating candy.

The second reason for sugar addictions is the fact that our culture practically worships sweets. Candy is portrayed as a highly desirable gift, even a symbol of love, and it is often used as a reward or a special treat. During many holidays, sweet foods are served as an integral part of the tradition. What would Christmas be without candy canes? What would Hanukkah be like without chocolate money? Halloween would not seem right without candy. In the Mexican-American culture the children are often thrilled to have a candy-filled piñata for their birthday party.

In addition to all this, candy is advertised on television, it is always placed within children's reach in supermarkets, and it is colorful and attractively wrapped. With this degree of exposure, cultural conditioning, and stimulation, it would be very surprising if children did not crave candy. It is impossible to say whether children would desire candy as much in the absence of all of this cultural emphasis on its desirability. I suspect that they would still eat it occasionally but not consider it qualitatively any different from carrots, bananas, crackers, or cheese.

In the following interview, a mother described to me her feelings and experiences with her three-year-old daughter's sugar addiction:

She used to be really into breastfeeding, she seemed to really enjoy that. With regular food, she doesn't seem to have that much of an interest unless it has sugar in it, and then there's a great interest in it. I feel real angry about the way that food's treated in this society. I'm continually having to deal with outside junk that she gets. I really resent having to go to the grocery store and have aisles and aisles of sugar stuff. I feel like sometimes going shopping gets to be a regular maneuver. Then, after I've carefully planned to avoid the aisles with the cookies or ice cream, I get up to the cash register, and I'm in some long line, and the whole time I'm in the line, I'm having to give her attention to get rid of the feelings like, "Mommy's saying no to the candy bar there." Then we get out of the grocery store, and there's the gum machine! And then at home on TV something sweet is being advertised constantly. We've had trouble trying to cope with the sugar stuff, and I'm not quite sure how well we always do on that. Sometimes I say, "Sure, I'll sit down and eat a candy bar with you" (laughter). I guess the main thing is just trying to make it so that you don't bring it into your home. That makes it a little easier, and trying to set up alternatives like encouraging them to eat fruit, and having good food around that's nutritious for them.

The authors of the book *Are You Hungry?* claim that children will come to regulate their own candy consumption once all restrictions are removed from candy, and once it is treated no differently from carrots or bananas (Hirschmann & Zaphiropoulos, 1985). The idea is that candy will be highly desirable only when it is saved for special occasions, used as rewards, or otherwise rationed and restricted. Once this is no longer the case, and children know they will always have an unlimited supply, they will lose their frantic and intense craving for candy and be free to select a balanced diet for themselves. Here is my experience with this approach:

After having carefully regulated my children's candy con-sumption for years, I had the courage to try letting them eat as much as they wanted. Sarah, who was six years old at the time, binged on candy for about two months. After that, to my amazement, she ate very little, even though candy was still readily available to her. She became more and more particular about the kind of candy she liked, and started saying that certain candy was "too sweet," or "smelled bad." Nicky, who was eleven years old when I began this approach, never binged on candy, but regulated himself quite reasonably from the start.

When sweets are overly restricted during childhood, this can backfire and lead to an overconsumption of them later on, when the child is older and no longer under daily parental supervision. A mother I interviewed related to me the negative effects of her own strict upbringing:

Candy and cookies were very strictly regulated in our home. I used to get in trouble for eating them. My mother never said, "Who ate the cookies?" but rather "Who *stole* the cookies?" It was that wonderful thing I could do to be naughty. To this day, if I see a cookie, I have to eat it. It's the criminal in me coming out. I have to see if I can get away with it. After church, when they have a pile of cookies out there, I can feel my adrenaline going all out, and I have to eat as many as I can get my hands on! I'm overweight now because I just gained 30 pounds over the Christmas season from all the sweets I ate.

How Can I Prepare My Child for a Dental Appointment?

When selecting a dentist for your child, try to find one who will allow you to be present in the room. Although many dentists claim to have strict rules banning parents from the room, some are willing to bend their rules when a parent approaches them calmly and confidently. If the dentist is reassured that you will not interfere with the procedures and that your child will be cooperative, he or she is more likely to let you stay with your child. You are not being overprotective. Children want and need their parents during new experiences and times of stress. In fact, people of all ages need support when doing something frightening. Dental and medical procedures are frightening because they are new experiences, and there is often physical pain or discomfort involved.

Once you have selected a dentist, arrange for a preliminary visit, if possible, during which the child can see the room and the equipment and meet the dentist. Also, try to find out exactly what procedures will be used during the child's upcoming appointment. An effective way to prepare your child for a dental appointment is to act out with him ahead of time the procedures that will be followed by the dentist. You can take turns being the dentist and the patient. Role-playing the visit in this manner allows your child to know exactly what to expect, and it can also provide an opportunity for the child to release anxiety through laughter. Anything that produces laughter will be beneficial, and the funnier you can make it, the better. There are a number of creative ways you can elicit laughter: you can pretend to cringe with fear when your child is the "dentist" and you are the "patient," or you can pretend to be a stupid dentist who doesn't know where the teeth are, and inspect your child's toes instead of his teeth.

Some parents hope to spare their children apprehension by not telling them they are going to the dentist. This leads invariably to a feeling of betrayal in the child, accompanied by anger and a loss of trust, and it can create anxiety when going to new places in the future. It is always better to tell the truth. The child need not be told weeks in advance, however. One day before the appointment is probably sufficient advance notice for young children. This allows time for the child to ask questions, express his feelings, and rehearse the visit through play, but it does not give him enough time to dwell on it or to build up a huge amount of apprehension. Here is my own experience:

> At five years of age, Sarah had to go to the dentist for a check-up and teeth cleaning after not having been to the dentist for a year. The previous year, she had refused to let the dentist clean her teeth. I assumed it was because I had failed to prepare her adequately for the visit. This time, I decided that she would arrive knowing exactly what to expect and be fully prepared. I told her about the appointment one day ahead of time, and asked her if she wanted to pretend going to the dentist. She eagerly joined me in a game in which we took turns being the

dentist. When I was the dentist, I emphasized the importance of keeping her mouth open and of holding very still. Then I pretended to polish her teeth with an electric polisher, and I made a funny noise. This caused her to laugh, so I made another noise, claiming that I couldn't remember what noise the machine actually made. Together we experimented with a number of different noises, none of which sounded right. But this kept her laughing continuously for about 15 minutes! The next day at her appointment she was extremely cooperative, held very still, and the dentist had no trouble cleaning her teeth.

How Can I Help My Child Cope with Vaccinations and Blood Tests?

The guidelines for preparing a child for a shot or blood test are similar to those for a trip to the dentist. Everything should be clearly explained ahead of time, as well as the reasons for the procedure. Even young children can grasp the idea of a vaccination if it is explained in concepts with which they are familiar. It is important to make it clear that the child has no choice about the medical procedure. This will make it easier to accept than if the child somehow feels that she has the power to change the situation. Nevertheless, in order for the child to have some sense of control over the situation, smaller choices can be offered. Perhaps the child can choose the time of day, or can select which parent will take her, or which arm to have the injection in.

Role-playing is also beneficial, with a toy syringe, if you have one. You can take turns giving a shot to each other, and do whatever causes your child to laugh the most. The idea of a sharp metal needle going into their body can be quite frightening to young children, but the anticipation is often worse than the shot itself.

Any crying before, during, or after the shot needs to be allowed, and the child should not be made to feel she is weak for crying. Doctors and nurses can be asked not to stop or distract the crying. This can be done in a friendly manner with a simple statement, such as, "She needs to know that it is okay for her to cry." This may even be a relief for doctors and nurses because they will realize that you are not expecting them to make your child happy.

Many adults want to stop a child's crying after a shot because they want the child to be happy. It is tempting to say, "That didn't hurt, did it?" or "It's all over, so what are you crying about?" or "Look at this toy." But the child has experienced a frightening and hurtful event, and needs to cry in order to get over it.

The following example describes a mother's successful preparation of her three-year-old son's injection:

> I decided I would tell him the day before, so that he would have time to cry about it if he wanted to. So I told him, and I made it clear that he had no choice. I explained about the bad disease he could get that could leave problems afterwards, and that some scientists had found this new vaccine that would help protect him. Well, he immediately said, "No, I'm not going to have it," and he cried for a half hour or so. We got out the doctor kit and one of his favorite stuffed animals, and pretended that the animal needed the shot, and we let the animal be upset and scared. I told him, "It's alright if you're scared. All you have to do is hold still so it can be over as fast as possible." He still kept saying, "I'm not going to have that injection." Well, the next morning, it was the first thing he mentioned when he woke up. He no longer said he would not have the injection, but rather, "I don't want to have the injection." I said again that it was really important and that he had to have it, and we talked about how long it would hurt. When the time came, I gave him a choice of whether he wanted papa or me or both to take him, and he chose me. On the way, in the car, he was very quiet at first, then said, "I'm really scared." And I said, "It's all right to be scared. But I'm going to be with you, and it's going to be over fast." I really expected, once we got there, that he would be crying in the car and would refuse to get out. But he didn't! He got out willingly and went in. Fortunately, we didn't have to wait any length of time. The nurse had the syringe in her pocket, so he never really saw it. I was holding him, and he had the injection, and it was over. He didn't cry until after the nurse had left, and then cried some.

How Can I Help My Child Deal with Physical Pain?

It is extremely distressing for parents to see their child in pain, and it is natural to want to do everything within their power to diminish the pain. One purpose of pain, however, is to draw our attention to the injured or diseased part of our body, so that we can release and express the feelings surrounding the pain and thereby become more relaxed. This relaxation will allow the blood to flow more easily to the diseased area and allow the tissues to repair themselves more quickly.

The spontaneous response of a child following an injury is to seek the attention of someone, get physically close, and cry. This crying needs to happen. To interrupt the crying with pain-killing medication is no different from interrupting crying of any other origin. The pain and fear have already occurred and need to be released. If allowed to cry as much as needed, the child's pain will eventually disappear of its own accord.

There is no need to protect children from the sensation of physical pain caused by minor injuries because their body is equipped to handle it. It is a part of their everyday life. In fact, it is part of their learning experiences about the world. When pain from an injury has been fully felt and expressed, the child will learn how to protect himself and take necessary precautions in the future. When the pain is immediately masked by pain killers, learning cannot take place as effectively.

A common response to children's bumps and bruises is to put ice on them. This only numbs the very area of the body that needs to be felt the most. Unless ice is necessary for medical reasons (in order to prevent or reduce swelling), a more helpful response would be to hold the child and touch the painful area gently while accepting the child's crying. Children instinctively touch or look at their injuries in an attempt to draw their attention to the pain. If the injury itself is too sensitive to be touched, then perhaps the surrounding skin can be gently touched. It is important to provide prompt medical treatment when needed for injuries, but this can be done while allowing the child to feel and express the pain.

Many parents have reported to me that, if they do not "make a big deal" of small injuries, their child does not cry very much, but if they give them full attention, affection, and sympathy, the crying goes on and on. They wonder if they are somehow causing their child to cry more than necessary. Children never cry more than necessary. Physical injuries involve not only physical pain, but also emotional pain that needs to be expressed: confusion, anger at the interruption, grief about the loss of play time, or fear of it happening again. These feelings cause a need to cry that may last much longer than the physical pain itself.

Children also make use of physical injuries to cry about other things: feelings of frustration, anger, or grief which have been accumulating. The scraped knee or the cut finger provides the pretext that allows stored-up tensions resulting from past hurts (both emotional and physical) to be released. Most children are able to cry after physical hurts, because a certain amount of this crying is tolerated and understood by parents. Prolonged crying after minor injuries is more likely to occur in children who have not had sufficient opportunity to cry regularly since birth. They are simply using the occasion to catch up. Children benefit from having someone "make a big deal" of their minor hurts, and who can encourage crying at these crucial times when the tears are readily accessible.

Some parents fear that they are teaching their child to be a cry-baby or become weak by "giving in" to minor pain. This is more likely to occur with a male child. The cultural expectation is for boys to "be tough" and withstand pain without complaining. This attitude is unfortunate. Crying is not an indication of weakness, but a source of health and strength. Men are more prone than women to stress-related illnesses, and they die at an earlier age. If boys were encouraged to feel pain and express it, perhaps they would live just as long as women.

How Can I Help My Child During a Trip to the Emergency Roon?

A medical emergency does not allow any time for careful preparation, as described in the preceding sections. You may have no way of knowing what medical procedures will be used. Young children cannot be expected to cooperate willingly with doctors and nurses under these conditions because they do not understand the reason for the examinations or treatments. It may be necessary to use force (but not violence) in order to hold a young child still.

The main guidelines are to explain as much as possible about what is happening, allow your child to cry, and stay with your child at all times, if possible. One of the most distressing experiences for young children is to be with strangers at a time when they are frightened and in pain.

The following example from a mother I interviewed illustrates the negative consequences of leaving a child alone with doctors and nurses during a medical emergency:

> One evening Richard was running and fell and hit his head on concrete. Later on he said he couldn't see well, and I got very concerned. Maybe he could have a hematoma or something. So I decided to take him to the emergency room. At the last minute, he didn't want to go. He was crying, saying he wasn't going. Well, I told him we had to. I said it may be nothing, but it might be serious. When we got there, there was a young physician on duty. Richard started crying and wouldn't let the doctor touch him. The doctor said to me, "We often get more cooperation when parents aren't in the room." Now everything in me said, "No, that's wrong. I can't leave." But I was also scared to death that something was seriously wrong with my child and was really at the point of being willing to do anything to make sure that it wasn't. So I went out. Of course, he continued to scream, and they had to call in an orderly to help hold him down. Finally, I opened the door and went back in. They had been able to see that he was okay. Well, he was angry at them and angry at me. I had deserted him. He didn't want me to hold him. And he hit me. He was just so angry that I had left

him. They said he seemed to be okay, and that we could go
home, but he had such a need to regain some control that he
refused to leave and began crying because we were leaving. He
didn't want to get in the car, and said, "I don't want to go home.
I want to live here." So I just waited while he cried some more.
Finally he got in the car. But when we got home, he did not want
to get out of the car. He stayed in there for about ten minutes,
crying, before he came into the house.

Although this mother was accepting of her son's crying and
raging, he would have had less to cry about if she had insisted on
staying with him in the emergency room. It is sometimes
extremely difficult to stand up for children's emotional needs in
situations such as these.

How Can I Help My Child Through a Stay in the Hospital?

In spite of the fact that most hospitals have now adopted
policies supportive of children's emotional needs, hospitalization
is still extremely confusing and stressful for young children
(Thompson & Stanford, 1981). There are several steps parents can
take to help their child through such an experience and minimize
the trauma involved:

1. Prepare your child ahead of time (if there is time). It has been
shown that advance preparation is effective in reducing children's
fears during hospitalization and surgery (Trawick-Smith &
Thompson, 1986). Explain everything that will be done and why.
Be honest about the possibility of physical pain. If the hospitalization is scheduled for a specific date in the future (a non-
emergency situation), try to arrange a visit to the hospital with
your child, to see where she will be staying and to meet some of
the nurses. At home, you can role-play the hospital stay, as
described above for a visit to the dentist, and provide opportunities for your child to play with toy medical equipment. Books
about children in hospitals can be quite helpful in providing
information and can be used as a starting point for questions and

open discussion about fears and concerns (Fassler, 1986). It is important to let your child ask questions, verbalize fears, and release feelings through laughter and crying.

In spite of careful preparations, children can still develop all sorts of misconceptions because of their limited information, their fears and fantasies. The most common misconceptions concern the reasons for hospitalization. Many children believe that their hospitalization is punishment for something they have done wrong or a rejection by their parents (Fassler, 1986). Anything that can be done to clarify the reasons for hospitalization will be beneficial in reducing the child's anxiety.

2. Let your child bring a special toy from home. It can be very reassuring to a child to have a familiar object when she is in a strange and frightening place.

3. Stay with your child as much as the hospital policy will allow. Many children's hospitals have realized that children need their parents during times of stress and now allow parents to sleep on a cot next to the child's bed. Try not to let yourself be intimidated by an efficient or impersonal atmosphere and feel free to stand up for your child's needs. There are places where you will not be allowed to go, such as surgical rooms, but you can let your child know that you will be with her afterwards. If you cannot be present the entire time, try to arrange for someone else to be with your child. Important times to be present are during the first night, before and after surgery, during any other major tests or procedures, and at bedtime.

4. Inform yourself and explain all procedures and treatments to your child as much as possible. When the reasons are not fully understood, operations can be felt as mutilations, and any therapeutic procedures can be greatly misinterpreted. If the child needs to be isolated because of an infectious disease, she may come to feel rejected or unclean. Restrictive diets may be experi-

enced as deprivations, and restriction of mobility can feel oppressive to children who do not understand the reasons.

The more clarification children receive, the less anxious and the more cooperative they will be. The younger the child, however, the less likely she will be to understand explanations. Because of this it is unrealistic to expect very young children (under the age of three or four years) to react positively to a nurse's interventions or to cooperate willingly (Bergmann, 1965).

5. Be vigilant and know your rights. You have the right to see your child's medical records and know who is examining her and why. You can question procedures that you feel are unnecessary. You can also check any medication given, and you can help the nurses by keeping an eye on any apparatus hooked up to your child to be sure it is working properly.

6. Let your child have as many choices as possible and as much control over what happens to her. There may be little choice at times, but any decision she can make herself will be beneficial in helping her to feel less of a victim and more in control of the situation. You can suggest to the nurse that your child be allowed to choose which arm to put intravenous fluid in or which finger to prick for a blood test. Perhaps she can be allowed a choice of foods. Children past infancy can certainly decide for themselves whether they need pain-killing medication.

7. Allow a release of feelings. Although loud crying may not be appropriate at times, especially if other patients are bothered by the noise, perhaps there is another room you and your child can go to if she needs to cry. It is extremely important for her to be able to do so. In extensive observations of children in a long-stay hospital, it was noted that those children who openly cried and screamed at the beginning subsequently adjusted very well to their hospital stay and became quite accepting of medical care and of the limitations imposed on them. This was in striking contrast to children who were so-called "perfect" patients right from the

start. Although these children appeared to be calm, cheerful, and cooperative, they were the ones most likely to show signs of stress later on, such as regression to infantile modes of behavior, wetting and soiling, eating or sleeping difficulties, and learning inhibitions. This indicates that the unrestrained discharge of fear, despair, and rage is a healthy and necessary outlet for children under distressing circumstances such as a hospital stay (Bergmann, 1965). Very sick children will probably not cry because all their energy goes towards healing the physical ailment. Once they are stronger, however, crying is likely to occur and can then be encouraged.

8. Touch and hold your child as much as possible. Physical contact is especially important during illness and pain. Stroking, massages, and hugs can be beneficial in accelerating the healing process. Holding your child's hand during an uncomfortable procedure can greatly help her feel confident and relaxed. If the child is experiencing physical pain, it is helpful to touch the area involved and allow the child to express her feelings.

9. Take care of yourself. Don't forget to eat and sleep, and find someone to talk to and cry with if you need to. It has been shown that when parents have an opportunity to express their feelings about their children's hospitalization, this has a positive influence on their children's emotional state as well as their own (Wolfer & Visintainer, 1975). Try to find other people your child knows well to be with her at times so you can take a break. Attending to a child's needs during a medical crisis can be extremely exhausting, both emotionally and physically. A mother I interviewed told me how she took care of her own need to cry in a hospital:

> Mary was only two-and-a-half years old when she had to have
> eye surgery. I was very upset when the nurse took her from me
> and wheeled her into the operating room, and I couldn't help
> sobbing. I felt the need for someone to be with me, to give me
> some caring attention while I cried. It was a Catholic hospital,
> so I asked for a nun. When she came, I asked her to be with me

and pray with me while I cried. We went to the chapel, and I cried for at least half an hour while she just held my hand. She said her prayer, and I said my prayer, each in our own way. After that I felt much better and went back and waited outside the operating room.

10. After your child is back at home, encourage a release of feelings about the hospital experience, as well as fantasy play about doctors, illness, surgery, and hospitals. Do not be surprised if your child cries and generally "makes a big deal" of any additional minor injuries or medical procedures after returning home. This is a common reaction in children who have undergone hospitalization and surgery. They are making use of the minor injury to release the distress associated with the previous major medical procedure. This is especially likely to occur if they were very cooperative and "brave" while in the hospital, with little display of strong emotions, if they were simply too sick to cry, or if it was physically painful for them to do so.

What Can I Do If My Child's Health Is Being Affected By Stress?

The causes of childhood stress have changed rapidly in recent years. In the past, childhood stress was caused primarily by inadequate housing and nutrition, forced labor, and strict and rigid upbringing with physical punishment in an environment where children were to be "seen and not heard." Nowadays more and more children are being stressed by such factors as divorce of parents and pressure to excel academically at an early age (Elkind, 1981). Many other sources of stress in young children's lives have been extensively researched, and are listed in Chapter 1 (Honig, 1986).

Stress can lead to symptoms of free-floating anxiety, which manifests itself as restlessness, irritability, unhappiness, and inability to concentrate. Stress can also cause a change in the function of body tissues, organs, and systems (Selye, 1956). These, in turn, can lead to a lowering of the body's resistance to disease (Rahe et al., 1964). Children under stress, who are not releasing tension through the discharge mechanisms of laughter, crying, and raging, may therefore become ill more often than children who are less stressed. Pediatricians are seeing an increase in stress-related stomachaches and headaches in children (Elkind, 1981).

If you think that your child's health is being adversely affected by stress, the first step is to determine the source of stress. Is his school or daycare too structured? Is her day too hurried? Does he need more individual attention? Is she watching too much TV? Is he being teased by other children? Does she have too many responsibilities? Sometimes the source of stress is not readily apparent from outside circumstances, and you may need to probe into your child's inner world of feelings. Does he have some new fears, misconceptions, or guilt feelings?

Once you have made every attempt to diminish the source of stress, you can help your child express feelings through talking, playing, laughing, crying, and raging, by following many of the suggestions in this book. Children will spontaneously keep themselves free of the effects of stressful experiences, provided they are allowed the freedom to cry and rage.

Children who are ill with the flu or other disease often make use of the increased attention from adults to release stored-up tensions and feelings. Do not be surprised if your child cries more readily during such illnesses. This is exactly what he needs to do. Any crying that occurs during an illness is beneficial. It may serve to dissipate tensions that helped contribute to the illness in the first place.

Is There a Cure for Bedwetting?

The age of five years is considered the dividing line between normal and possibly problematic bedwetting that would require medical evaluation (American Psychiatric Association, 1980). If your child urinates in bed at night after his fifth birthday, this could be an indication of either physical or psychological problems (Rowan, 1974).

Possible physical causes for bedwetting include anatomical malformations (which require surgery) and allergies. However, the physical causes of bedwetting account for only a small percentage of the total. Ninety-eight percent of bedwetters have no organic disease or defect that could account for the problem (Azrin & Besalel, 1979).

There is some evidence that bedwetting can be caused by repressed emotions. It has been observed that bedwetters are often children who do not express their feelings openly. In the book *Windows to Our Children*, it is stated that these children, if they did not wet the bed, might have asthma or eczema (Oaklander, 1978).

Bedwetting is more common in children who have been labeled "hyperactive" (Stewart et al., 1966). This is not surprising, since both bedwetting and hyperactivity can result from stored-up tensions that have not been released. Of relevance, too, is the fact that bedwetting is more common in boys than in girls. At age five, 7% of boys and only 3% of girls are bedwetters (American Psychiatric Association, 1980). This may be related to the fact that the expression of feelings in boys is almost totally unacceptable in our culture. Boys are under pressure to be tough, strong, and competitive, and often have no choice but to repress their fears and other painful feelings. In her book *Growing Up Free* (1980), Pogrebin suggests that bedwetting is a direct result of these sex-role pressures on boys.

If your child is a bedwetter, the first thing to do is obtain a complete medical evaluation to rule out the possibility of physical causes. If the problem seems to be psychological, you can try letting your child sleep with or near you. A feeling of closeness and safety at night may eliminate the problem. If he still wets the bed, you can try to determine causes of stress and anxiety in his life. Are his days overly structured? Is he being pushed to succeed academically or in sports? Is he being pressured to strive for perfection in other areas? Is he allowed to express his feelings? Does he admit being scared at times? Is he able to cry and rage freely when anxious or frustrated? Parents often think that boys should be taught to be brave and deny their fears, but there is nothing unmasculine about being scared. Boys are first and foremost human beings, and they deserve to feel and express the entire range of human emotions. Their health and sanity depend on it.

Sometimes bedwetting begins during obvious times of stress or change, such as a move to a new home, the birth of a sibling, or following hospitalization. Every effort should be made to help the child express his feelings verbally, through play and laughter, and by crying and raging. Whatever the cause of bedwetting, it is *never* helpful to tease, scold, humiliate, threaten, or punish the child. Bedwetting is involuntary, and children would stop doing it if they could.

It is normal for parents of bedwetters to experience feelings of guilt, shame, anxiety, resentment, and even anger at the child, and these feelings may need an outlet before a parent can be helpful (Oaklander, 1978). If you are struggling with a bedwetting problem in your family, you will greatly benefit by sharing your feelings openly with an attentive listener who can remain objective and supportive without trying to judge your situation or give you advice.

What If My Child Is Hyperactive?

The current official label for hyperactive children is "Attention Deficit Disorder with Hyperactivity," and the symptoms include: difficulty paying attention, impulsivity, and excessive activity that appears to be haphazard and poorly organized. Such children are restless, careless, fidgety, and easily distracted (American Psychiatric Association, 1980). Much has been written and speculated about hyperactivity, and several causes have been suggested, including neurological problems or "minimal brain dysfunction" (Millichap, 1975) and allergies to food additives (Feingold, 1975).

As with any problem, the approach most likely to succeed is a holistic one in which all possible causes are taken into account, including a child's diet as well as emotional and environmental factors. Drugs should be given only as a last resort, if at all, after all other approaches have been tried. Although neurological disorders have been claimed to justify the use of drugs that affect the nervous system, such disorders are not substantiated in the vast majority of cases of children given drugs for hyperactivity. A diagnosable neurological disorder has been found to be associated with Attention Deficit Disorder in only 5% of the cases (American Psychiatric Association, 1980). Drugs deal only with the superficial symptoms, merely masking the problems (Sroufe & Steward, 1973), and their use deprives the child of a sense of powerfulness or control over his own life (Oaklander, 1978). Furthermore, when drugs are used, both the parents and the child come to believe that the hyperactivity is a physical dysfunction. Although this can relieve feelings of guilt, it may also tend to make the family believe there is little hope for a cure. This can adversely affect the long-range consequences of this kind of treatment (Whalen & Henker, 1976).

It is quite possible that many cases of hyperactivity are caused by stored-up tensions resulting from painful feelings. Crying can become repressed during the first few years through jiggling, rocking, and other forms of movement. If this is a frequent parental response to a baby who needs to release tensions by crying, the baby can eventually begin to feel the need to provide his own movement stimulation when he is feeling upset. A high activity level can become a chronic control pattern that effectively holds his feelings in check, just as eating or thumb sucking can become a control pattern in another child. As this pattern continues into the preschool years, such a child is likely to be labeled "hyperactive" as soon as he is in a school situation.

Hyperactivity is ten times more common in boys than in girls (American Psychiatric Association, 1980). It has also been shown that parents typically provide more movement stimulation for their infant sons than for their infant daughters (Fagot & Kronsberg, 1982). Although it is fun and important for babies to be rocked, jostled, and actively played with, great care must be taken not to use this kind of stimulation to distract a baby from his need to cry. The movement stimulation has not necessarily been excessive, it may simply have been provided at the wrong times, resulting in a suppression of crying.

If your child has been labeled hyperactive, this does not necessarily mean that he has any more problems than a child who is overweight or who sucks his thumb. It does not mean that you have failed as a parent. Movement may simply be his way of coping with stress and avoiding painful feelings. Anything you can do to encourage him to express his feelings (especially through crying and raging) is likely to diminish his hyperactive symptoms. (See Chapter 1 for suggestions of ways to encourage crying.) It may be necessary to use firm and calm holding at times, in order to stop wild, frantic, and aggressive movements, and help him begin channeling his energy into crying and raging. (See Chapters 5 and 6 for examples of the use of holding.)

Many children are labeled hyperactive when in fact this is their normal and healthy activity level. Schools often expect children as young as four or five years of age to sit still for long periods of time and attend to tasks that are not of their own choosing. Some children are naturally more active than others and need more freedom than is allowed. For such children this kind of school will be particularly hard to tolerate. (As mentioned in Chapter 3, it is inappropriate to demand this of *any* child under eight years of age.) Before assuming that your child really is hyperactive, it may be wise to find another school that allows more freedom of movement.

Exercises

Explore your childhood.

1. How did you feel during mealtimes as a child? Were you ever forced to eat a food that you did not want, or denied a food that you did want? How did you feel about that?

2. How did you feel about going to the doctor or dentist as a child? What memories do you have associated with doctors?

3. Do you remember being sick as a child? How did you feel while you were sick?

Express your feelings about your child.

1. How do you feel about your child's current food preferences? How do you feel about trusting your child's self-selection of foods?

2. How do you feel when you take your child to a doctor or dentist? Is there anything that makes this difficult for you?

3. Does your child have any ailments that you feel may be caused by stress? Is your child hyperactive or a bedwetter? If so, how do you feel about this?

Nurture yourself.

1. Treat yourself to a food that was forbidden or restricted during your childhood. Enjoy it!

2. Do you have a food addiction or weight problem? If so, join a support group that addresses eating problems.

3. Do something to take care of your health. Some suggestions: a) Make a change in your diet. b) Get more exercise. c) Get a medical check-up. d) Begin seeing a therapist.

CONCLUSION

There are four important themes running throughout this book.

Young children have intense needs. Children's needs are not always fully recognized in our culture. Young children require a great deal of individual attention from caring adults, time and space to play, continuity in caretakers, and a stimulating environment. They need to be listened to, read to, and played with. Their exposure to the adult world must be in doses they can assimilate.

Young children have intense feelings. Children experience the entire range of human emotions, from minor irritations to intense anger, fear, grief, and confusion. They are sensitive and vulnerable. Frustration is frequent as children attempt to learn new skills and have their needs met. Fears are common because of lack of information, children's growing imagination, and new awareness of death. Jealousy between siblings can occur even in the most loving of families.

Young children can heal themselves of painful experiences. Human beings are born with the ability to recover from experiences of loss, fright, confusion, and frustration. The recovery process is the release that occurs through crying, raging, trembling, talking, playing, and laughing. Children must be allowed full expression of their painful feelings. They would not be able to flourish if we accepted only their positive feelings and ignored or punished their spontaneous expressions of pain, discomfort, frustration, outrage, or fear. We must offer them an environment that can accept their entire range of emotions, whatever the intensity. Once these painful feelings have had a harmless outlet, children will be free to experience the pleasant feelings of love, happiness, and self-confidence that we desire for them.

Unacceptable behavior is not a sign of inherent wickedness. Children are not born with a desire to hurt others or to make life difficult for their parents. Sometimes, however, they do act in ways that are unacceptable and harmful to themselves or others. One of the most difficult challenges parents face is to deal with unacceptable behavior without imposing needless pain or damaging their relationship with the children. This book describes ways of helping children develop acceptable and cooperative behavior without the use of either rewards or punishments. There are only three reasons that children "misbehave:" 1) They are experiencing a need, 2) They lack information, or 3) They have painful feelings such as fear, anger, or grief resulting from past experiences of hurt or frustration.

The approach to parenting described in this book may seem to be extremely difficult and time-consuming to carry out in practice. You may feel that you have better things to do than sit with your children until they fall asleep, tolerate a half hour of angry crying, or play doctor with them. It is easy to become impatient with young children and to wish our lives with them could be simpler. Good quality time spent with young children is not wasted time, although it may feel that way. By filling children's needs when they are young you will give them a solid foundation of self-esteem and provide them with valuable skills for coping with life.

While you are striving to give your children good attention, remember to take care of your own needs and to share your parenting responsibilities with other adults. Be sure to ask for help when you need it. It is easy to become burnt out when trying to be a good parent because our culture neither recognizes nor supports the valuable work that parents do.

As you experience the ups and downs of early childhood with your children, remember that these years do not last forever. Before you know it, your children will be grown. There will come a time when they will brush their teeth without being reminded, eat without spilling, and read to themselves. As they grow they will naturally want to spend more time with friends and less time with you. Your children are dependent on you now in ways that will soon change. Cherish your moments of togetherness and remember to enjoy the playfulness, spontaneity, intensity, sense of wonder, curiosity, and eagerness of your young child.

If you feel guilty after reading this book because you wish you had acted differently when your children were younger, rest assured that it is never too late to alleviate whatever pain your children may have experienced in the past. Parenting is a process of growth and change. Your parenting style will change, not only as your children develop, but also as you yourself mature as a person. You have always done your very best with the information and resources you had at the time. It will be helpful if you can express your guilt feelings and then appreciate yourself as the caring parent you have always been.

If children can be helped to flourish, then the entire world will flourish and become the place we all yearn for. People will be loving and respectful of each other. We will take good care of our beautiful planet and use its resources wisely. Nobody will live in poverty. War will become a thing of the past because people will know how to resolve their conflicts in peaceful ways. We will use our brilliant minds to discover ever more exciting facts about our universe.

We can make all this come true!

REFERENCES

Allan, J. Use of holding with autistic children. *Special Education in Canada*, 1977, 51, 11-15.

American Psychiatric Association: *Diagnostic and Statistical Manual of Mental Disorders*, Third Edition. Washington, D.C., 1980.

Armstrong, L. *Kiss Daddy Goodnight: A Speak-Out on Incest*. New York: Hawthorn Books, Inc., 1978.

Armstrong, T. *In Their Own Way*. Los Angeles: Jeremy Tarcher, Inc., 1987.

Axline, V.M. *Play Therapy*. Ballantine Books, 1969.

Azrin, N.H., & Besalel, V.A. *A Parent's Guide to Bedwetting Control*. Pocket Books, 1979.

Bandura, A., Ross, D., & Ross, S.A. Imitation of film-mediated aggressive models. *Journal of Abnormal Psychology*, 1963, 66, 3-11.

Baruch, D. W. *New Ways to Discipline*. New York: McGraw-Hill, 1949.

Baumrind, D. Current patterns of parental authority. *Developmental Psychology Monographs*, 1971, 4, 1-103.

Bayley, N., & Schaefer, E.S. Correlations of maternal and child behaviors with the development of mental abilities: Data from the Berkeley Growth Study. *Monographs of the Society for Research in Child Development*, 1964, 29 (Serial No. 97).

Bergmann, T. *Children in the Hospital*. New York: International University Press, 1965.

Bettelheim, B. *The Uses of Enchantment*. New York: Alfred A. Knopf, 1975.

Bowlby, J. *Separation: Anxiety and Anger.* New York: Basic Books, 1973.

Bradley, R.H., & Caldwell, B.M. The relation of infants' home environment to mental test performance at fifty-four months: A follow-up study. *Child Development,* 1976, 47, 1172-1174.

Bredekamp, S. (Ed.). *Developmentally Appropriate Practice in Early Childhood Programs Serving Children From Birth Through Age Eight.* National Association for the Education of Young Children, Washington, D.C., 1988.

Bronson, G.W. Fear of visual novelty: Developmental patterns in males and females. *Developmental Psychology,* 1970, 2, 33-40.

Brown, N.S., Curry, N.E., & Tittnich, E. How groups of children deal with common stress through play. In *Play: The Child Strives Toward Self-Realization.* National Association for the Education of Young Children, Washington, D.C., 1971.

Bruner, J.S. Play is serious business. *Psychology Today,* January 1975, 81-83.

Burton, S.G., Calonico, J.M., & McSeveny, D.R. Effects of preschool watching on first-grade children. *Journal of Communication,* 1979, 29, 3.

Bushnell, D.D. The cathartic effects of laughter: Mood, heart rate, and peripheral skin temperature. (Doctoral dissertation in Sociology, University of California, Santa Barbara, 1979).

Caplan, F., & Caplan, T. *The Power of Play.* New York: Anchor Press/Doubleday, 1973.

Chesler, P. Women as psychiatric and psychotherapeutic patients. *Journal of Marriage and Family,* November 1971, 750.

Cline, F. *Understanding and Treating the Severely Disturbed Child.* Evergreen Consultants in Human Behavior. Evergreen, Colorado, 1979.

Cline, V.B., Croft, R.G., & Courrier, S. Desensitization of children to television violence. *Journal of Personality and Social Psychology,* 1973, 27, 360-365.

Cousins, N. *Anatomy of an Illness as Perceived by the Patient: Reflections on Healing and Regeneration.* New York: Norton, 1979.

Crepeau, M.T. A comparison of the behavior patterns and meanings of weeping among adult men and women across three health conditions (Doctoral dissertation, University of Pittsburgh, 1980). *Dissertation Abstracts International,* 1981, 42, 137.

Davis, C. Self-selection of diet by newly weaned infants. *American Journal of Diseases of Children,* 1928, 36, 651-679.

Doust, J.W.L., & Leigh, D. Studies on the physiology of awareness: The interrelations of emotions, life situations, and anoxemia in patients with bronchial asthma. *Psychosomatic Medicine,* 1953, 15, 292-311.

Elkind, D. The case for the academic preschool: Fact or fiction? In Smart & Smart (Eds.), *Preschool Children: Development and Relationships.* The MacMillan Company, 1973.

Elkind, D. *The Hurried Child: Growing Up Too Fast Too Soon.* Addison-Wesley, 1981.

Emerson, W.R. Infant and child birth re-facilitation. Human Potential Resources, 4940 Bodega Ave., Petaluma, CA 94952, 1984.

Emerson, W.R. Psychotherapy with infants and children. *Pre and Perinatal Psychology Journal,* 1989, Vol. 3(3).

Eron, L.D. Relationship of TV viewing habits and aggressive behavior in children. *Journal of Abnormal and Social Psychology,* 1963, 67(2), 193-196.

Faber, A., & Mazlish, E. *Siblings Without Rivalry.* New York: W.W. Norton & Co., 1987.

Fagot, B.I. Consequences of moderate cross-gender behavior in preschool children. *Child Development,* 1977, 48, 902-907.

Fagot, B.I., & Kronsberg, S.J. Sex differences: biological and social factors influencing the behavior of young boys and girls. In S.G. Moore & C.R. Cooper (Eds.), *The Young Child: Reviews of Research* (Vol. 3). National Association for the Education of Young Children, Washington, D.C., 1982.

Fassler, D. The young child in the hospital. In J.B. McCracken (Ed.), *Reducing Stress in Young Children's Lives.* National

Association for the Education of Young Children, Washington, D.C., 1986.

Feingold, B.F. *Why Your Child is Hyperactive.* New York: Random House, 1975.

Finkelhor, D. *Sexually Victimized Children.* New York: The Free Press, 1979.

Frankl, V.E.(Ed.) *Psychotherapy and Existentialism: Selected Papers on Logotherapy.* New York: Washington Square Press, 1967.

Frey II, W.H., & Langseth, M. *Crying: The Mystery of Tears.* Winston Press, 1985.

Furman, E. Helping children cope with death. In J.B. McCracken (Ed.), *Reducing Stress in Young Children's Lives.* National Association for the Education of Young Children, Washington, D.C., 1986.

Garvey, C. *Play.* Cambridge, MA: Harvard University Press, 1977.

Gelfand, D.M. Social withdrawal and negative emotional states: Behavior therapy. In B.B. Wolman, J. Egan, & A.O. Ross (Eds.), *Handbook of Treatment of Mental Disorders in Childhood and Adolescence.* Englewood Cliffs, NJ: Prentice-Hall, 1978.

Gilmartin, B.G. The case against spanking. *Human Behavior,* February 1979, 18-23.

Ginott, H.G. *Group Psychotherapy with Children: The Theory and Practice of Play Therapy.* New York: McGraw-Hill, 1961.

Ginott, H.G. *Between Parent and Child: New Solutions to Old Problems.* New York: The MacMillan Co., 1965.

Goranson, R.E. Media violence and aggressive behavior: A review of experimental research. In L. Berkowitz (Ed.), *Advances in Experimental Social Psychology* (Vol. 5). New York: Academic Press, 1970.

Gordon, T. *Parent Effectiveness Training.* New American Library, 1975.

Graham, O.T., & Wolf, S. Pathogenesis of urticaria. *Psychosomatic Medicine,* 1950, 13, 122.

Green, R. One hundred ten feminine and masculine boys: Behavioral contrasts and demographic similarities. *Archives of Sexual Behavior,* 1976, 5, 425-446.

Growing Without Schooling. Bi-monthly journal published by Holt Associates, 2269 Massachusetts Avenue, Cambridge, MA 02140.

Guerney, B.G., Guerney, L.F., & Andronico, M.P. Filial therapy. In C. Shaefer (Ed.), *The Therapeutic Use of Child's Play.* New York: Aronson, 1976.

Heron, J. *Catharsis in Human Development.* Human Potential Research Project, Department of Adult Education, University of Surrey, Guildford, Surrey GU2 5XH, United Kingdom, 1977.

Hirschmann, J.R., & Zaphiropoulos, L. *Are You Hungry? A Completely New Approach to Raising Children Free of Food and Weight Problems.* A Signet Book, New American Library, 1985.

Hitz, R., & Driscoll, A. Praise or encouragement? New insights into praise: Implications for early childhood teachers. *Young Children,* 1988, 43(5), 6-13.

Hodgson, R.J., & Rachman, S. An experimental investigation of the Implosion Technique. *Behavioral Research and Therapy,* 1970, 8, 21-27.

Hoffman, M.L., & Saltzstein, D. Parent discipline and the child's moral development. *Journal of Personality and Social Psychology,* 1967, 5, 45-57.

Honig, A.S. Stress and coping in children. In J.B. McCracken (Ed.), *Reducing Stress in Young Children's Lives.* National Association for the Education of Young Children, Washington, D.C., 1986.

Honig, A.S. Humor development in children. *Young Children,* 1988, 43(4), 60-73.

Holt, J. *Teach Your Own.* Dell Publishing Co., Inc., 1981.

Holt, J. *How Children Learn.* Dell Publishing Co., Inc., 1983.

Holt, J. *Freedom and Beyond.* Pinchpenny Press, 1984.

Hyson, M.C. Lobster on the sidewalk: Understanding and helping children with fears. In J.B. McCracken (Ed.), *Reducing Stress in*

Young Children's Lives. National Association for the Education of Young Children, Washington, D.C., 1986.

Jackins, H. *Elementary Counselors Manual for Beginning Classes in Re-Evaluation Co-Counseling.* Seattle: Rational Island Publishers, 1970.

Jackson, S.A. Should you teach your child to read? *American Education,* October 1977, 13(8), 27-29.

Janov, A. *The Feeling Child.* New York: Simon & Schuster, 1973.

Janov, A. *Imprints: The Lifelong Effects of the Birth Experience.* New York: Coward-McCann, Inc., 1983.

Joseph, S.M. *Children in Fear.* New York: Holt, Rinehart & Winston, 1974.

Karle, W., Corriere, R., & Hart, J. Psychophysiological changes in abreaction therapy. Study I: Primal Therapy. *Psychotherapy: Theory, Research and Practice,* 1973, 10, 117-122.

Klaus, M.H., & Kennell, J.H. *Maternal-Infant Bonding.* St. Louis: The C.V. Mosby Company, 1976.

Koblinsky, S., Atkinson, J., & Davis, S. Sex education with young children. In J.B. McCracken (Ed.), *Reducing Stress in Young Children's Lives.* National Association for the Education of Young Children, Washington, D.C., 1986.

Kohn, A. *No Contest: The Case Against Competition.* Boston: Houghton Mifflin, 1986.

Kostelnik, M.J., Whiren, A.P., & Stein, L.C. Living with He-Man: Managing superhero fantasy play. In J.B. McCracken (Ed.), *Reducing Stress in Young Children's Lives.* National Association for the Education of Young Children, Washington, D.C., 1986.

Kreitler, H., & Kreitler, S. Children's concepts of sexuality and birth. *Child Development,* 1965, 37, 363-378.

Kuhlman, R.L. *Humor and Psychotherapy.* Dow Jones-Irwin, 1984.

Lazarus, A.A. The use of systematic desensitization in psychotherapy. In H.J. Eysenck (Ed.), *Behavior Therapy and the Neuroses.* London: Pergamon, 1960.

Lefkowitz, M.M., Eron, L.D., Walder, L.O., & Huesmann, L.R. *Growing up to Be Violent: A Longitudinal Study of the Development of Aggression.* New York: Pergamon Press, Inc., 1977.

Lepper, M.R., Greene, D., & Nisbett, R.E. Undermining children's intrinsic interest with extrinsic reward: A test of the overjustification hypothesis. *Journal of Personality and Social Psychology,* 1973, 28(1), 129-137.

Levitin, T. An overview of the effects of divorce on children: Problems, questions, and perspectives. *The Psychiatric Hospital,* 1983, 14, 149.

Liebert, R.M., Neale, J.M., & Davidson, E.S. *The Early Window: Effects of Television on Children and Youth.* New York: Pergamon Press, 1982.

Loewald, E. The development and uses of humour in a four-year-old's treatment. *International Review of Psychoanalysis,* 1976, 3, 209-221.

Lovaas, O.I. Effect of exposure to symbolic aggression on aggressive behavior. *Child Development,* 1961, 32, 37-44.

MacFarlane, J.W., Allen, L., & Honzik, M.P. A developmental study of the behavior problems of normal children between 21 months and 14 years. *University of California Publications in Child Development* (Vol. 2). Berkeley: University of California Press, 1954.

Madsen, M.C. Developmental and cross-cultural differences in the cooperative and competitive behavior of young children. *Journal of Cross-Cultural Psychology.* 1971, 2, 365-371.

Magid, K., & McKelvey, C.A. *High Risk: Children Without a Conscience.* New York: Bantam Books, 1987.

Masson, J.M. *The Assault on Truth: Freud's Suppression of the Seduction Theory.* New York: Farrar, Straus & Giroux, 1984.

Maurer, A. What Children Fear. *Journal of Genetic Psychology,* 1965, 106, 265-277.

McLoyd, V.C. Scaffolds or shackles? The role of toys in preschool children's pretend play. In G. Fein & M. Rivkin (Eds.), *The Young Child at Play.* (Reviews of Research, Vol. 4).National

Association for the Education of Young Children, Washington, D.C., 1986.

Miller, A. *For Your Own Good: Hidden Cruelty in Child-Rearing and the Roots of Violence.* New York: Farrar, Straus & Giroux, 1983.

Miller, A. *Thou Shalt Not Be Aware: Society's Betrayal of the Child.* Meridian Books, New American Library, 1984.

Miller, L.C., Barrett, C.L., Hampe, E., & Noble, H. Factor structure of children's fears. *Journal of Consulting and Clinical Psychology,* 1972, 39, 264-268.

Miller, L.C., Barrett, C.L., Hampe, E., & Noble, H. Comparison of reciprocal inhibition, psychotherapy, and waiting list control for phobic children. *Journal of Abnormal Psychology,* 1972, 79, 269-279.

Millichap, J.G. *The Hyperactive Child With Minimal Brain Dysfunction.* Chicago: Year Book Medical Publishers, Inc., 1975.

Moffat, M.J., & Painter, C. *Revelations: Diaries of Women.* New York: Random House, 1974.

Moody, R.A. *Laugh After Laugh: The Healing Power of Humor.* Headwaters Press, 1978.

Newson, J., & Newson, E. *Four Years Old in an Urban Community.* London: Allen & Unwin, 1968.

Oaklander, V. *Windows to Our Children.* Moab, Utah: Real People Press, 1978.

Orlick, T. *The Cooperative Sports and Games Book.* Pantheon Books, 1978.

Orlick, T. *The Second Cooperative Sports and Games Book.* Pantheon Books, 1982.

Osborn, D.K., & Endsley, R.C. Emotional reactions of young children to TV violence. *Child Development,* 1971, 42, 321-331.

Pearce, J.C. *Magical Child.* New York: E.P. Dutton, 1977.

Pellegrini, A.D. Communicating in and about play: The effect of play centers on preschoolers' explicit language. In G. Fein & M. Rivkin (Eds.), *The Young Child at Play.* (Reviews of Research, Vol 4). National Association for the Education of Young Children, Washington, D.C., 1986.

Pepler, D. Play and creativity. In G. Fein & M. Rivkin (Eds.), *The Young Child at Play*. (Reviews of Research, Vol. 4). National Association for the Education of Young Children, Washington, D.C., 1986.

Piaget, J. *The Psychology of Intelligence*. London: Routledge & Kegan Paul, Ltd., 1950.

Piaget, J. *Play, Dreams and Imitation in Childhood*. New York: W.W. Norton & Company, 1962.

Piaget, J. *The Child's Conception of Number*. New York: W.W. Norton & Company, Inc., 1965.

Pierce, R.A., Nichols, M.P., & DuBrin, J.R. *Emotional Expression in Psychotherapy*. New York: Gardner Press, 1983.

Pines, M. Invisible playmates. *Psychology Today*. September, 1978, 38.

Pogrebin, L.C. *Growing Up Free: Raising Your Child in the Eighties*. New York: McGraw Hill, 1980.

Radin, N. Childrearing antecedents of cognitive development in lower-class preschool children. *Dissertation Abstracts International*, 1970, 30, 4364B. (University Microfilms No. 70-4170).

Rahe, R.H., Meyer, M., Smith, M., Kjaerg, G., & Holmes, T.H. Social stress and illness. *Journal of Psychosomatic Research*, 1964, 8, 35-44.

Riley, C.M., Day, R.L., Greeley, D.M., & Langford, W.S. Central autonomic dysfunction with defective lacrimation. I. Report of five cases. *Pediatrics*, 1949, 3, 468-478.

Rothbart, M.K. Laughter in young children. *Psychological Bulletin*, 1973, 80, 247-256.

Rowan, R.L. *Bed-Wetting: A Guide for Parents*. New York: St. Martin's Press, 1974.

Rubin, K.H., & Everett, B. Social perspective-taking in young children. In S.G. Moore & C.R. Cooper (Eds.), *The Young Child*. (Reviews of Research, Vol. 3). National Association for the Education of Young Children, Washington, D.C., 1982.

Rubin, K.H., & Howe, N. Social play and perspective-taking. In G. Fein & M. Rivkin (Eds.), *The Young Child at Play*. (Reviews of

Research, Vol. 4). National Association for the Education of Young Children, Washington, D.C., 1986.

Rush, F. *The Best Kept Secret: Sexual Abuse of Children.* New Jersey: Prentice-Hall, 1980.

Rutter, M. *Helping Troubled Children.* New York: Penguin Books, 1975.

Ryan, B.H. Would you free your children from the monster? *Denver Post,* June 9, 1974.

Salt, R. & Salt, E. Pretend play training and its outcomes. In G. Fein & M. Rivkin (Eds.), *The Young Child at Play.* (Reviews of Research, Vol. 4). National Association for the Education of Young Children, Washington, D.C., 1986.

Schaefer, C.E. Play Therapy. *Early Childhood Development and Care,* 1985, 19, 95-108.

Schaefer, C.E., & O'Connor, K.J. (Eds.) *Handbook of Play Therapy.* New York: John Wiley & Sons, 1983.

Scheff, T.J. *Catharsis in Healing, Ritual and Drama.* University of California Press, 1979.

Schofield, W. *Psychotherapy: The Purchase of Friendship.* New York: Prentice-Hall, 1964.

Schram, W., Lyle, J., & Parker, E. *Television in the Lives of Our Children.* Stanford University Press, 1961.

Sears, R.R., Maccoby, E.E., & Levin, H. *Patterns of Child Rearing.* Row, Peterson, 1957.

Seliger, S. What is best for the children? *Working Mother,* April 1986, 77-78.

Selnow, G.W., & Bettinghaus, E.P. Television exposure and language development. *Journal of Broadcasting,* Winter 1982, 26(1), 469.

Selye, H. *The Stress of Life.* New York: McGraw-Hill, 1956.

Selzer, J.G. *When Children Ask About Sex.* Boston: Beacon, 1974.

Shostak, M. *Nisa: The Life and Words of a !Kung Woman.* Vintage Books, 1983.

Simkin, P. Siblings at birth. *Mothering,* Fall 1987, 45, 61-67.

Simon, W., & Gagnon, J.H. Psychosexual development. In J. Heiss (Ed.), *Family Roles and Interaction.* Chicago: Rand McNally, 1976.

Smith, R.E. The use of humor in the counterconditioning of anger responses: A case study. *Behavior Therapy,* 1973, 4, 576-580.

Solter, A. *The Aware Baby: A New Approach to Parenting.* Goleta, California: Shining Star Press, 1984.

Sroufe, L.A., & Steward, M.A. Treating problem children with stimulant drugs. *The New England Journal of Medicine,* August 23, 1973, 289(8), 407-413.

Stewart, M.A., Pitts, F.M., Craig, A.G., & Dieruf, W. The hyperactive child syndrome. *American Journal of Orthopsychiatry,* 1966, 36(5), 861-867.

Straus, M.A. Some social antecedents of physical punishment: A linkage theory interpretation. *Journal of Marriage and the Family,* 1971, 658-663.

Terr, L.C. Play therapy and psychic trauma: A preliminary report. In C.E. Schaefer & K.J. O'Connor (Eds.), *Handbook of Play Therapy.* John Wiley & Sons, 1983.

Thompson, R.H., & Stanford, G. *Child Life in Hospitals: Theory and Practice.* Springfield, Illinois: Charles C. Thomas, 1981.

Trawick-Smith, J., & Thompson, R.H. Preparing young children for hospitalization. In J.B. McCracken (Ed.), *Reducing Stress in Young Children's Lives.* National Association for the Education of Young Children, Washington, D.C., 1986.

Ude-Pestel, A. *Betty.* Palo Alto: Science & Behavior Books, 1977.

Vener, A.M., & Snyder, C.A. The preschool child's awareness and anticipation of adult sex-roles. *Sociometry,* 1966, 29(2), 159-168.

Ventis, W.L. Case history: The use of laughter as an alternative response in systematic desensitization. *Behavior Therapy,* 1973, 4, 120-122.

Vygotsky, L.S. Play and its role in the mental development of the child. *Soviet Psychology,* 1967, 5, 6-18.

Waal, N. A special technique of psychotherapy with an autistic child. In F. Caplan (Ed.), *Emotional Problems of Early Childhood.* New York: Basic Books, 1955.

Watson, J.B., & Rayner, R. Conditioned emotional reactions. *Journal of Experimental Psychology,* 1920, 3, 1-14.

Weissglass, J., & Weissglass, T.L. *Learning, Feelings and Educational Change. Part I: Overcoming Learning Distress.* Santa Barbara, California: Kimberly Press, 1987.

Whalen, C.K., & Henker, B. Psychostimulants and children: A review and analysis. *Psychological Bulletin,* 1976, 83, 1113-1130.

Winn, M. *The Plug-In Drug.* New York: Viking Press, 1985.

Winn, M. *Unplugging the Plug-In Drug.* Penguin Books, 1987.

Woldenberg, L., Karle, W., Gold, S., Corriere, R., Hart, J., & Hopper, M. Psychophysiological changes in feeling therapy. *Psychological Reports,* 1976, 39, 1059-1062.

Wolfer, J.E., & Visintainer, M. Pediatric surgical patients' and parents' stress responses and adjustments as a function of a psychological preparation and stress point nursing scale. *Nursing Research,* 1975, 24, 244-255.

Yablonsky, L. *Psychodrama: Resolving emotional problems through role-playing.* New York: Basic Books, 1976.

Yachnes, E. The myth of masculinity. *American Journal of Psychoanalysis,* 1973, 33(1), 58.

Zaslow, R.W., & Breger, L. A theory and treatment of autism. In L. Breger (Ed.), *Clinical-Cognitive Psychology: Models and Integrations.* New Jersey: Prentice-Hall, 1969.

INDEX

Abandonment, 12, 37, 40

Abuse: and neglect, 135, 141; physical, 10; sexual, 10, 42, 59, 149, 166-172; verbal, 10

Academic skills, 77, 80, 91-92, 197

Achievements, 75, 161, 197

Acting out behavior, 17-18, 160

Activity level, 201, 202

Addictions, 83, 183-186

Advertisements, 85, 87, 124, 184, 185

Aggressiveness: and hyperactivity, 202; and spanking, 120-121; in boys & men, 70-71, 73, 83; in children, 19, 26, 59, 100, 132, 165; towards siblings, 152-155

Alcoholism, 10

Allergies, 199, 200

Altruism, 93

Amusement parks, 55

Anger: and laughter, 27, 107, 137, 154; and play, 107; in boys versus in girls, 73; in adults, 10, 31, 32-34, 69, 88, 139, 163, 169, 200; in children, 12, 16-19, 22-23, 30, 44, 59, 122, 123, 132, 152-154, 159, 164, 173, 187, 191, 192; in stepchildren, 173-174

Animals, 12, 37, 38, 42, 43, 47, 53, 54, 78, 144

Anxiety (see also Fear): and laughter, 102, 172, 187; caused by punishment, 10, 120-121; in children, 37, 41, 69, 79, 152, 172, 174; in parents, 10, 31, 140, 161, 200; of separation, 36, 42, 57-61; sources of, 12, 41, 187, 197

Apologizing, 16, 32

Appetite, 168

Approach/avoidance phenomenon, 53

Art work, 30-31, 70

Assimilation, 63, 93-96, 99, 106-109, 150, 172

Asthma, 8, 199

Hobbies, 63-64, 111
Holding: babies, 14, 37, 70,
   182; children during
   illness, 196; children while
   crying, 14, 135-136, 146;
   hyperactive children, 202;
   need for, 11, 37; violent
   children, 17, 135-136, 154,
   165
Holidays, 184
Home-schooling, 82
Homophobia, 71
Homosexuality, 71-72
Hopelessness, 44
Hormones, 7, 8, 170
Hospitalization: of child,
   192-197, 200; of mother,
   37, 59, 97, 99, 145
Housework, 111, 142-144
Humiliation, 10, 119, 167
Humor, 103, 160
Hunger, 125, 129, 179, 183
Hunter-gatherers, 57, 156
Hurried child, 161, 197-198
Hurts: as source of tension,
   13, 191, 201; during
   parents' childhoods, 9; by
   commission, 10-11, 15-16,
   42, 139-142; by omission,
   11; by parents, 9, 171, 182;
   carried over from infancy,
   12-13, 58-59, 135;
   situational, 11-12, 15
Hygiene, 172
Hyperactivity, 26, 146, 199,
   200-202

Identification with parents,
   174
Ignoring, 13, 19, 25, 31
Illness: and food, 179, 180;
   and hospitalization,
   193-197; and pain, 11, 177,
   196; and repression of
   crying, 19, 191; crying
   during, 196, 198; of a
   parent, 12, 37, 40, 59, 97,
   99, 140, 145; stress-
   related, 14, 177, 191,
   197-198
Imaginary playmates, 100
Imagination, 41, 42, 78, 84,
   104, 108
Imitation, 79, 95, 142
Impatience, 9-10, 42, 60,
   205
Implosive technique, 46
Impulses, 10, 118
Impulsivity, 200
Incest, 167, 170-171
Incubators, 58
Independence, 60, 71, 138,
   145, 161
Infancy (see Babies)
Infections, 194
Information: about death, 48,
   65-67; about sex, 67-69,
   150, 172; about violence,
   48, 65, 82; assimilating,
   63, 93-96, 99, 106-109,
   150, 172; giving children,
   47, 52, 53, 80, 122,
   133-134, 166, 193; lack of,

RESOURCES

Associations and Agencies Helping Parents, Families, and/or Young Children

Family Resource Coalition
(Information, listings of support groups, & a newsletter)
230 N. Michigan Age., Suite 1625
Chicago, IL 60601

Coalition for Children and Youth
(An information center)
815 15th St., N.W.
Washington, DC 02192

National Committee for Prevention of Child Abuse
332 S. Michigan Ave., Suite 950
Chicago, IL 60604

International Society for Prevention of Child Abuse and Neglect
1205 Oneida St.
Denver, CO 80220

Parents Anonymous
(Support for parents concerned about abusing their children)
6733 S. Sepulveda, Suite 270
Los Angeles, CA 90045

Parents United
(Assistance to families affected by child sexual abuse)
P.O. Box 952
San Jose, CA 95108

Fatherhood Project
c/o Bank Street College of Education
610 W. 112th St.
New York, NY 10025

Mothers at Home
P.O. Box 2208
Merrifield, VA 22116

Parents Without Partners
8807 Colesville Rd.
Silver Spring, MD 20910

Parents Sharing Custody
435 N. Bedford Dr., Suite 310
Beverly Hills, CA 90210

The Box Project
(Pairs families in need with helper families)
Box 435
Plainville, CT 06062

Home School Legal Defense Association
P.O. Box 950
Great Falls, VA 22066

Growing Without Schooling
Holt Associates
(Publishes a newsletter)
2269 Massachusetts Ave.
Cambridge, MA 02140

National Coalition on Television Violence
P.O. Box 2157
Champaign, IL 61820

Parenting in a Nuclear Age
c/o Bananas
6501 Telegraph
Oakland, CA 94609

National Organization of Mothers-of-Twins Clubs
12404 Princess Jeanne, N.E.
Albuquerque, NM 87112

Children in Hospitals
31 Wilshire Park
Needham, MA 02192

National Information Center for Handicapped Children and
Youth
P.O. Box 1492
Washington, DC 20013

Therapies and Growth Movements that Help Adults Release Feelings Through Laughter, Crying, and Raging

Some of these offer counseling, classes, or workshops worldwide, while others are more localized. (This is simply a listing, not a personal endorsement by the author.)

Radix Institute (Reichian Therapy)
Rt. 2, Box 89-A
Granbury, TX 76048

International Institute for Bioenergetic Analysis
144 E. 36th St.
New York, NY 10016

Rolf Institute
P.O. Box 1868
Boulder, CO 80306

The Primal Institute
2215 Colby Ave.
Los Angeles, CA 90064

Rebirthing
P.O. Box 8269
Cincinnati, OH 45208

Gestalt Therapy Institute
337 South Beverly Drive, Suite 206
Beverly Hills, CA 90212

Re-Evaluation Counseling
P.O. Box 2081, Main Office Station
Seattle, WA 98111

The Center for Feeling Therapy
1017 South La Brea
Los Angeles, CA 90019

Feeling-Expressive Therapy
The Therapy Center
247 Park Ave.
Rochester, NY 14607

ABOUT THE AUTHOR

Dr. Solter is a developmental psychologist living in Santa Barbara, California. She has a Master's degree in human biology from the University of Geneva, Switzerland, where she studied with the Swiss psychologist, Dr. Jean Piaget. Her Ph.D. in psychology was earned in 1975 at the University of California in Santa Barbara. She has taught introductory psychology at the University of California, done original research, and is the author of several scientific publications. Her first book, *The Aware Baby: A New Approach to Parenting* (Shining Star Press, 1984) has been sold around the world and translated into German and French. In addition to writing, Dr. Solter teaches classes and conducts workshops for parents.

ORDER FORM

Helping Young Children Flourish
by Aletha J. Solter. Ph.D.

To order copies of *Helping Young Children Flourish,* ($11.95), just fill out the form below, enclose a check or money order made out to Shining Star Press, and send to:

> Shining Star Press
> P.O. Box 206
> Goleta, CA 93116
> U.S.A.

> **Shipping:** Books will be shipped free of charge anywhere in the U.S. Foreign orders: Add $1.00 per copy for shipping. Payment must be in U.S. dollars by money order or a draft on a U.S. bank. Allow 30 days in the U.S. and up to 120 days to foreign addresses.

> Please inquire about our discount rates for bulk orders.

Please send me _____ copies of *Helping Young Children Flourish.*

_____ copies at $11.95 each . . . . $_____ . _____

California residents add 72¢ sales tax per book . . . . $_____ . _____

Shipping fee (see above) . . . . $_____ . _____

Total amount enclosed . . . . $_____ . _____

To be shipped to:

Name _____

Street _____

City _____ State (or _____ Zip _____
                        country)

243

ORDER FORM

The Aware Baby: A New Approach to Parenting
by Aletha J. Solter. Ph.D.

To order copies of *The Aware Baby: A New Approach to Parenting* ($9.95), just fill out the form below, enclose a check or money order made out to Shining Star Press, and send to:

> Shining Star Press
> P.O. Box 206
> Goleta, CA 93116
> U.S.A.

> **Shipping:** Books will be shipped free of charge anywhere in the U.S. Foreign orders: Add $1.00 per copy for shipping. Payment must be in U.S. dollars by money order or a draft on a U.S. bank. Allow 30 days in the U.S. and up to 120 days to foreign addresses.

> Please inquire about our discount rates for bulk orders.

Please send me _____ copies of *The Aware Baby: A New Approach to Parenting.*

_____ copies at $9.95 each .... $_____ . ____

California residents add 60¢ sales tax per book .... $_____ . ____

Shipping fee (see above) .... $_____ . ____

Total amount enclosed .... $_____ . ____

To be shipped to:

Name _____

Street _____

City _____ State (or _____ Zip _____
                         country)

245